# THE KITCHEN
# LINENS BOOK

*Other books by EllynAnne Geisel*

*The Apron Book: Making, Wearing,*
*and Sharing a Bit of Cloth and Comfort*

*Apronisms: Pocket Wisdom for Every Day*

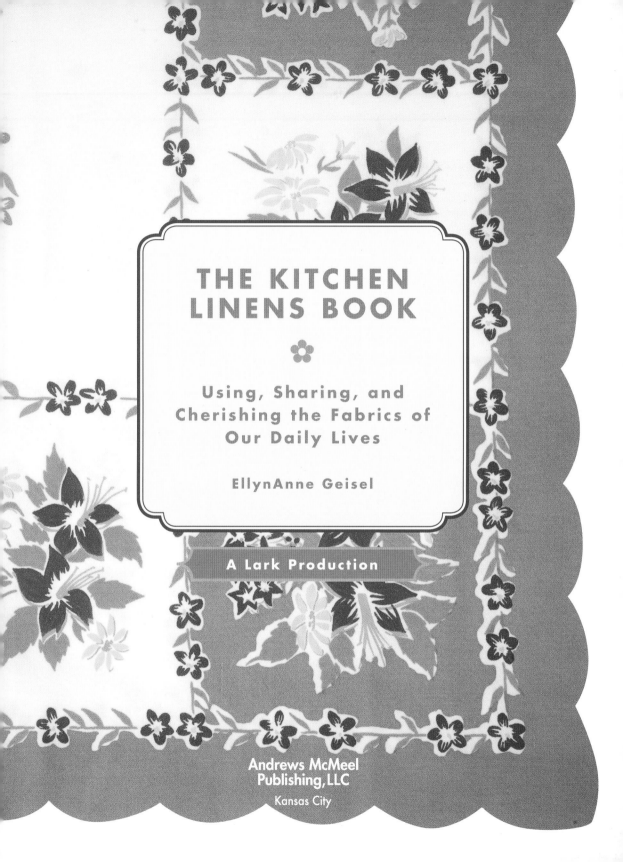

# THE KITCHEN LINENS BOOK

## Using, Sharing, and Cherishing the Fabrics of Our Daily Lives

EllynAnne Geisel

A Lark Production

Andrews McMeel
Publishing, LLC
Kansas City

# THE KITCHEN LINENS BOOK

09 10 11 12 13 WKT 10 9 8 7 6 5 4 3 2 1

ISBN-13: 978-0-7407-7763-9
ISBN-10: 0-7407-7763-7

Library of Congress Cataloging-in-Publication Data
Geisel, EllynAnne.
  The kitchen linens book : using, sharing, and cherishing the fabrics of our
daily lives / EllynAnne Geisel. -- 1st ed.
      p. cm.
  "A Lark production."
  Includes bibliographical references.
  ISBN-13: 978-0-7407-7763-9
  ISBN-10: 0-7407-7763-7
  1.  Household linens. 2.  Table setting and decoration. 3.  Kitchens--
Equipment and supplies.  I. Title.

  TX315.G45 2009
  646.2'1--dc22
                              2008032622


Book design by Diane Marsh

www.andrewsmcmeel.com

## ATTENTION: SCHOOLS AND BUSINESSES

Andrews McMeel books are available at quantity discounts with bulk purchase
for educational, business, or sales promotional use. For information, please
write to: Special Sales Department, Andrews McMeel Publishing, LLC,
1130 Walnut Street, Kansas City, Missouri 64106.

# CONTENTS

# FROM WHOLE CLOTH

**TO MY** way of thinking, a tablecloth is where all that defines us as family begins.

Just think for a minute about what takes place on and around the kitchen or dining room table. It's where all our family dramas, major and minor, tend to unfold. It's where we prop our elbows and talk, or sit up straight and dine. It's where we sort through the mail, dash off a note, make a to-do list, or chat on the phone with a friend. It's where the day begins and often ends, and where all that occurs in between gets discussed and revisited.

Personally, I love the whole ritual of laying out a freshly laundered cloth. I love the sensation of putting it down and patting it out. In that simple motion I feel connected to all the women before me, all the wives and mothers and homemakers who, like me, took delight in setting out a good meal or gathering loved ones around. I like to layer my cloths, choosing them with an eye to startling mixes of color and pattern and texture. It's as though I'm setting a stage, one with infinite dramatic possibilities for an ever-changing cast of characters.

My vintage kitchen linens, like my aprons, speak of past generations, but they also inspire me to think of future gatherings. It's an ongoing dialogue, really: they have stories to tell and I have chapters to add. Whenever I'm prowling my favorite haunts for second-hand finds, I listen for this conversation. The hand towel or napkin or tablecloth or hot pad that has the most to say is invariably the one I buy.

It's possible my love for kitchen linens stems from having so few as I was growing up. We were a large family, and the eight of us ate at a pecan-wood dining table. It was one of those furniture sets from the 1950s, Pledged within an inch of its life. Tablecloths were only for holidays, to my mother's way of thinking. I don't fault her for thinking that way. Opera inspired my mother, and classical piano sonatas. Not table linens.

Although I didn't inherit any cloths from my mother, I did come by a wonderful assortment from my mother-in-law. Hank's mother came from Germany and, along with Hummels, she collected cloth: bright tablecloths and fine damask and linen napkins and dish towels embroidered or crocheted along the edges. She'd set even her dinette in cloth, including the napkins. Which is at odds with who she was, in many respects: She and Hank's father lived very frugally, after immigrating to America. They saved everything for Hank's future, doing with less so that he could one day have more. If there hadn't been the war, and she hadn't had to escape her country and leave behind all that was dear and familiar, who knows who she would have become? I like to think that there was a hidden side of her, more colorful, lighter in step, because that's what I glimpse when I look at her linens.

Her collection may well have sparked my passion for all things cloth. More to the point, however, it was her daily use of her linens that influenced how I enjoy my own collection. And with my environmental awareness heightened, I'm practicing a less wasteful lifestyle by replacing paper goods with those of vintage cloth.

Besides, laundry has gotten so easy, with all sorts of wrinkle-free cycles. I rarely iron my everyday cloths. I just fluff and fold or put them right back on the table or towel rod.

Whatever I'm not using, I arrange in a glass-front china cabinet whose shelves allow me to display my linens like art. Some of my kitchen towels, table napkins, and aprons are in drawers, to be sure. But nothing is *put away*, to be preserved for future generations, because that to me is missing the point. If my future daughters-in-law and grandchildren ever come to treasure these kitchen linens of mine, it'll be because they remember them in constant use. Every stain, every sign of wear will be like a photograph, capable of summoning up certain people, occasions, or outings from their past. That's what happens whenever I see the pinkish blot on my mother's one good cloth, a damask that my sister Susan inherited. My father made that stain slurping a loaded spoonful of borscht, a soup he touted as a delicacy, but which we kids labeled disgusting. My mother always tried to hide the stain under a plate because she couldn't get it out completely. But far from ruining the cloth, that bit of spilled soup is what makes the cloth dear to both my sister and me. It's the Daddy Stain. To look at it is to summon him in a way no photograph can.

Aside from using, displaying, or otherwise enjoying my collection, however, I abide by no other rules. I put holiday dish towels in the kitchen in July and set the dining table with picnic napkins on a dreary day in November. I might start with a quilt and layer on cloths from two different eras, or unfurl my latest geometric find from the thrift shop and play it up with a blend of disparate place mats and napkins. The joy of my collection is in mixing and matching its pieces. I aim to surprise and delight, shock, and amuse.

With this book, as with *The Apron Book*, I hope to trigger *your* memories—and catalyze new ones. Somebody, someday, may cherish these pieces of mine for both the history they captured and the history they helped create. But for the time being, let's delight in them together.

# part one

# BE IT EVER SO HUMBLE

*The washing of dishes does seem to me the most absurd and*
*unsatisfactory business that I ever undertook.*
*If, when once washed, they would remain clean forever*
*and ever (which they ought in all reason to do, considering*
*how much trouble it is), there would be less occasion*
*to grumble; but no sooner is it done, than it requires*
*to be done again. On the whole, I have come to the*
*resolution not to use more than one dish at each meal.*
—Nathaniel Hawthorne (1844), while Mrs. Hawthorne was away

**LINENS THAT** stay in the kitchen—dish towels, breakfast cloths, appliance covers, place mats, and hot pads—are, by nature, more humble than their dining room counterparts. They're the workhorses of the household, after all, made to endure the indignities of floury hands, bacon-greased griddle handles, gravy-rimmed roasting pans, and messy eaters.

Maybe because they have borne witness to so much family life, however, kitchen linens hold a special place in our hearts. I remember one holiday season taking a selection of my hot pads and aprons to a senior-housing facility, where I was to give a talk about my collection. I strung up clotheslines in the dining room and reception area and then, using clothespins, hung each pad and apron for display. The female residents got very emotional gazing upon these reminders of their more vigorous days. Here they were, in an assisted-living environment, slow-gaited on walkers and canes,

with hearing aids and thick glasses, but they wanted me to know that *they* had once gotten up at dawn to put the turkey in for Thanksgiving; that *they* had welcomed a bevy of relatives and friends to their table; that *they* knew how to make gravy without lumps and pineapple upside-down cake in an iron skillet. One look at a crocheted hot pad or an embroidered apron unlocked years of happy memories as mistress of the household.

I feel that way about my own vintage kitchen linens collection, although I acquired most of it not for the articles' historic value, but simply because I'm drawn to them—their vibrant colors, their bold graphics, their charming handwork, and their utility.

## KNOW YOUR FIBERS

COTTON is the soft fiber, found in the seedpod of cotton plants, that is spun into thread and yarn. The longer the fiber, the better the quality of cotton.

FLAX fibers, derived from flax or linseed plants, are used to produce linen, a durable and absorbent fabric. Linen production dates back thousands of years to Egypt, where flax was first actively cultivated.

RAMIE fibers originate in the bark of the stalks of ramie plants, native in eastern Asia. The fibers are often blended with cotton or wool for durability. Since processing the fibers is difficult and expensive, ramie is not used widely in commercial textiles.

RAYON, or viscose, as it is known in Europe, is produced from cellulosic fiber, usually derived from wood pulp. Though rayon is man-made (a process patented in 1894), it is not technically a synthetic fiber, since it comes from naturally occurring polymers. Soft, smooth, and highly absorbent, rayon can be made to imitate silk, cotton, linen, and wool fabrics. When it first appeared in fabrics at the turn of the century, it was considered "artificial silk."

SILK is the protein fiber unwound from the cocoons of cultivated silkworms. Silk fabrics were first produced in China between 6000 and 3000 BC.

WOOL fiber is derived from the fur of animals, mainly sheep; these fibers are highly elastic and absorbent and create fabrics that are bulkier and retain more heat than other textiles.

# *Mondays*
## ARE FOR WASHING

With everything today machine made, any linen featuring genuine handwork is a real treasure and gets snapped up by collectors. Day-of-the-week (DOW) kitchen towels are especially fun to collect and, of course, use.

They often began as plain cotton weave, purchased as yardage and then cut and hemmed. Toweling yardage was also available with striping, usually in red and blue. The edging and striping was of a tighter weave than the rest of the fabric. Once the towel was hemmed, a homemaker would apply a transfer pattern and embroider on top of it. Some of the more famous makers of transfers are Walker's, which produced hot-iron transfers as early as 1879; Vogart, a main source for day-of-the-week designs; Aunt Martha's, another DOW source since the 1930s; and the Butterick Publishing Company, the giant sewing pattern manufacturer, whose original February 1945 kitchen motif is reproduced and included in the back of this book, by special arrangement with the McCall's Pattern Company.

The blue-edged kitten towel caught my friend Andrea Pitt's eye at an antique store, and she bought it strictly because the embroidery was so cute. The adorable Kewpie doll towels belong to my friend Jan Means—a thousand times, I wish I'd discovered that set first. The set stands out not only because of the darling design, but also for its red-striped edge.

Many of my own DOW purchases feature Scottie dogs, which led me to ponder why this particular dog was so popular a transfer. It was probably Franklin Roosevelt who brought the English-bred dog to the public's attention in the 1930s; fabric motifs and transfer designs would have picked up on the trend. I learned that these Scottie

DOW towels do indeed date to the late '30s or '40s by speaking to Stephani Paige at DeWitt and Company in Nebraska. The Scottie transfer, she recalls, was part of a bundle of like-packaged transfers she bought from a woman having a farm sale in the little town of Palmer, Iowa. Another farm wife at the sale remembered loving the "little doggie designs" so much, she embroidered four sets of towels.

Now that kitchen towels like these are making a huge comeback, reproductions are readily available. Reproductions may be advertised as true vintage, but the endearing details of the originals, such as the obvious unevenness of hand hemming and embroidery, will be replaced with the perfection of machine stitchery. Sellers of antique textiles tell me also to be wary of linen advertised as vintage that's packaged in a matching cloth envelope—a sure sign it's not bona fide.

# How to Apply a Transfer

*Note:* *The vintage transfer included in this book may be used only once.*

1. Set dry iron to "Linen" setting (350 degrees). Allow iron to reach proper temperature or transfer may not work.
2. Place protective cloth over ironing board to keep excess ink from staining ironing board cover.
3. Place fabric on ironing board, right side up, over the protective cloth.
4. Place transfer face down on fabric.
5. Place a clean sheet of paper directly over the transfer so that the entire inked surface is covered.
6. Press firmly and evenly in slow, circular motion for 30 seconds, no longer. BE CAREFUL TO HOLD TRANSFER IN ONE PLACE TO AVOID SMEARING.
7. Allow to cool for at least one minute before removing paper.

For more hot-iron transfers of vintage designs, check out some of these online sources:

www.sewingpalette.com

www.colonialpatterns.com

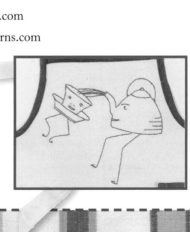

**HOT PADS**. Pot holders. Hot plates. Trivets. Some are for grasping pans hot from the oven or stove, others are for protecting your table from scorching-hot platters and such. To me, however, they're all hot pads, because I use them interchangeably. I'll grab a couple of Dresden Plate pads at a time to take a pie out of the oven, even though I know they were probably pieced for a quilt, originally.

Still, I do recognize that some were specifically crafted as trivets, to protect a table's surface from oven-hot casseroles. The crocheted grape clusters, for instance—inside each grape is a cork-lined bottle cap. And some of my friend Robin Wright's crocheted hot pads have a lip on the underside to encase a "burner pad," a cardboard thing that clearly had insulating properties. That's what I love about the women who made these: they'd take a thing meant for one use (the burner pads were supposed to go on stove burners, to keep a glass coffee carafe, say, from cracking), and fashion them to serve another useful purpose.

# Making Hot Pads

*I* was a madwoman for making hot pads, growing up. I'd make them with those loops you'd weave on a little square loom, and I used to time myself to see how quickly I could turn one out. The loops came in a big bag and they were cotton rag—which did not stretch, by the way. The tricky part was when you'd finished the weaving and had to take the pad off the loom: The whole thing could unravel if you weren't careful while working the edge. I'd get to that third side and my spindly fingers would interlock those loops until I had myself just the one loop left for hanging the pad on a hook. We had more pads in our kitchen than we could use in a lifetime, but that didn't stop me from "loomin'" more. I loved to work out the designs and then choose the colors.

Pot holder looms became popular in the 1930s as a way to use textile remnants. Packaging on the cotton-loop looms manufactured in the 1950s shows women enjoying the craft, even making it a social occasion. Today, the loom and bags of loops are sold as a diversion for young children, although of course anyone can make them. Look for looms and bags of cotton or synthetic loops (no longer woolen sock remnants!) in discount and craft stores, as well as online. The sturdiest looms, made from steel, are still available online from some of the original manufacturers, including Wool Novelty Co.

Hot-pad looms really do make the best hot pads, provided you don't use synthetic loops. They're just the right size, shape, and density, and can be tossed in the wash without shrinking or unraveling. Making them brings instant gratification, no matter how old you are. You can use your fingers to weave the loops, or a large crochet hook. Here's how to finish them:

### traditional method

Starting at one corner of the loom, detach two consecutive loops from their pegs. Using your fingers or a crochet hook, pull the second loop through the first loop. Bring the third loop off its peg and pull it through this loop; continue in this manner around the loom, detaching loops as you go, until you've got one loop left and the entire pad is off the pegs.

### fringe finish

Without removing your weaving from the loom, carefully place the foot of your sewing machine at the upper right-hand corner of the woven area. You'll want to position it so that the needle pierces the loops just outside the weaving. Sew down the right side, stop at the corner, lift the foot, turn the corner, and resume, stitching all the edges until you've reached your starting point. Remove from the sewing machine; remove the pot holder from the loom. Using cotton embroidery floss, embroider over the machine stitching with a simple chain stitch.

**BRIGHT, BEAUTIFUL** kitchen linens got their start in the Depression, really. That's when even the wealthiest women, who were raised to oversee kitchen help, found them-selves, of necessity, in the kitchen by themselves, doing all the cooking and cleaning up because they could no longer afford help. The better-off families had kitchens equipped with a few conveniences—a gas stove and a refrigerator, say—but most women faced an enormous task when it came to food preparation. Everything had to be prepared from scratch; you could buy a loaf of bread ready-made, but little else. Women toiling over a hot sink or stove truly appreciated a bit of cheer in the way of vibrantly colored and fancifully designed dish towels.

And it wasn't just dish towels that took on color and verve during the Depres-sion: Tablecloths, too, got a lot more interesting, as meals became less formal affairs. Dinner might still be served on the white damask in the dining room, but with Mother doing all the cooking and serving, it was inevitable that breakfast and lunch migrated to the kitchen—or more specifically, to a little room or alcove off the kitchen called the breakfast nook. The nook housed a square or gate-legged table that was surrounded by a couple of chairs or built-in benches. Conventional tablecloths would have been way too big for this cozy setup, so the breakfast cloth was invented.

## from the linen closet
### Patty Bedard

*E*ven before I went into the business of liquidating estates, I purchased furniture, china, and linens that once belonged to someone else. There's something about an antique and its owner having had a history together that interests me, and nowhere do I find this historical linkage more captivating than through a household's textiles.

Opening the drawers of a bureau to discover pressed and folded dining finery, or a kitchen cupboard to find neat stacks of brightly colored midcentury cloths and napkins, or a hall closet to come upon embroidered sheets, duvets, and exquisitely sewn hand towels—I feel like an archaeologist. It is with difficulty that I don't take everything home with me, rather than sell it to someone who couldn't possibly love each piece as much as the real owner nor care for it as a valued antiquity.

I believe in using all the linens I do bring home. When it's my turn to host the bridge group, I first set the tables with estate cloths, then I'll coordinate the dishes, stemware, and flowers to the coverings. I love pulling out my collection of silver napkin rings, arranging the seating with place cards, and in general fussing on behalf of my guests.

My children haven't expressed an interest in inheriting my linens. "They need ironing?" they'll say. "Are you kidding me?" So, I'm teaching my grandchildren the importance of genteel entertaining, by covering their play table with an embroidered cloth or showing them how to stick with a single color when picking the decorations for the dog's surprise birthday party. I hope they're listening, or all the histories that I've been safeguarding will suffer the fate of a thrift store.

**I HAVE** several of these breakfast cloths, all of them about 30 inches square. Few of them date back to the '30s, but they do embody the advice printed as far back as a 1917 recipe booklet of mine: "Even the simplest meal seems to taste better if the table is attractive."

I couldn't agree more. Even those faded from use and laundering can dispel the gloom of a winter morning, lighten the dread of a math test, and raise the spirit, or at least the eyelids, of sleepy heads. For breakfast, I love to put out this cotton cloth that my mother-in-law embroidered. How she found the time to complete a project like this is a mystery to me: she worked full-time alongside her husband in their corner

grocery, and yet managed to hand hem the edges, add a length of crochet, tack bright red rick-rack to that, and crochet a scalloped finish. The napkins, which are also her handiwork, feature little naked figures with vegetable heads—an odd pairing, but then she was probably utilizing scraps of cloth and transfers with one more "iron" to them. I appreciate her thriftiness, and the fastidiousness of women like her who took the time to finish their work so carefully. My breakfast cloths are over fifty years old, and none are fraying or ragged.

# Feed-Sack
## FINDS

**C**otton feed-bag cloth was a material much loved by thrifty women and farmers' wives, who recycled the colorful, absorbent sacking into towels, tablecloths, aprons, frocks, slips, bloomers, and infant layettes well into the '40s. The cloth you see here I purchased as sacking from Pandora's, an antique shop in Electra, Texas. What

made it such a good find was that the chain-stitched holes were still visible where the fabric had once been sewn closed. I couldn't bear to cut into it because of those holes. I could just see the homemaker removing the string to use in another manner. Combining scraps for the border, I carefully joined the two fabrics, making sure the little holes remained visible, and covered the seam with rickrack, the sunniest of embellishments.

**AFTER THE** Depression, women were hungry for more worldly fabrics and cloths. Department stores and mail-order catalogs offered toweling by the yard, as well as finished tablecloths and kitchen linens. Manufacturers like Weil & Durrse, Leacock, and Callaway Mills were producing designs with blues and purples that didn't fade, with mint and moss green that didn't run (a vast improvement over so-called fugitive dyes, which had been the norm), and with bold, contrast-y color combinations. By putting a halo of white around color-saturated motifs (a technique called "grinning"), they could print yard after yard of cloth without the dyes misaligning. See the cherry-bordered print above as an example of this halo effect. I just love the fruit borders, the huge clusters of roses, the wide plaids, and the eye-popping color combinations that these manufacturers produced until World War II redirected their efforts.

## BLUEBERRY-COCONUT MUFFINS

THESE BLUEBERRY muffins are my favorite breakfast surprise to make and serve. I mix the batter the night before and refrigerate it, adding the berries in the morning. Yes, I have to get up earlier on a muffin morning, but the smiles that greet this unexpected treat are worth it.

I've baked these muffins for over twenty years, following a recipe that is written on a piece of plain white paper; where I copied it from, I have no recollection. I'm sure I was attracted to the recipe because Hank loves blueberries, and it looked easy to accomplish.

½ cup (8 tablespoons/1 stick salted) butter, softened

¾ cup sugar

2 teaspoons freshly grated lemon zest

2 large eggs

5 tablespoons heavy cream

1 cup all-purpose flour

½ cup sweetened flaked coconut

½ cup blueberries

*SERVE FRESH-BAKED MUFFINS in a cloth-lined basket. Use a cheery print.*

Preheat the oven to 350°F. Butter and flour nine muffin cups.

In a bowl, using an electric mixer at medium speed, beat together the butter, sugar, and zest until fluffy.

Beat in the eggs one at a time.

At low speed, beat in the cream, then the flour until just combined.

Stir in the coconut, then gently fold in the blueberries.

Spoon the mixture into the prepared muffin cups. Bake until the edges are golden brown, about 25 minutes. Invert onto a rack and let cool.

This recipe can also be baked in mini loaf pans. It freezes well, too.

## from the linen closet
### *Lisa DiMona*

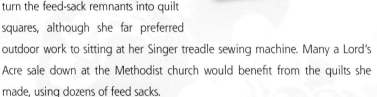

In 1930s rural Virginia, cows and hogs were fed with grain that came in sacks made out of different patterned cloth. With three daughters in the house, my grandfather knew to let his girls choose the livestock feed based on the colors or floral prints they loved, because once the sack was empty its fabric might become a dress for the church picnic or a new blouse for the first day of school. Grandma would also turn the feed-sack remnants into quilt squares, although she far preferred outdoor work to sitting at her Singer treadle sewing machine. Many a Lord's Acre sale down at the Methodist church would benefit from the quilts she made, using dozens of feed sacks.

We thought the quilt tops were the extent of her needlecraft, given how Grandma favored collecting acorns in the woods over stitching squares at her table. But she did produce these sweet little red and green patchwork place mats for my mother, and today, they are in my linen closet. Putting them out for Christmas breakfast with my kids, I note their simplicity and am reminded of the kind of sewing my grandmother liked to do: just a little bit.

**A LOT** of my prize dish towels date from the '30s and '40s. I bought them as panels for my apron designs—and then got them home, unwrapped them, and realized they were just too pretty to cut up. They're linen or a blend of linen and cotton, and you can't beat them for lint-free absorbency. Drying towels like this were once called "tea towels," not because they were used for tea, but because the mistress of the house used them to dry her fine bone china tea service. A drying towel stays in the kitchen unless I want to guarantee its safety from stains. Any towel that's embellished—embroidered, or edged, or painted—I'll put out in the powder room, where I can be fairly certain they'll be spared of hands greasy from food prep or dirty from tinkering with the mower. I like to use flour sacking for kitchen towels, because it's so absorbent and utilitarian—and usually big enough that I can fold it over and use it as a hot pad if necessary.

# WHAT MAKES A TOWEL
## . . . a Towel?

*I*f you've ever tried to blot up a spill with one of those polyester napkins that restaurants feature, you know that some fabrics just aren't cut out for the job. Thirstiness in a towel depends on three things: fiber content, weave, and finishing.

The best dish towels are made of linen. Not only is flax-derived linen the most absorbent vegetable fiber, it's also the strongest. A towel made of linen, or mostly linen, won't leave lint on your glassware, is naturally resistant to bacteria, and even when damp will still have some drying power, as it can absorb 20 percent of its weight in water. Cotton towels are also a terrific choice: They soak up spills, wring out readily, and don't wrinkle as easily as linen.

Good homemakers would insist on having linen towels for drying dishes, and cotton towels for drying hands.

The best weaves for toweling maximize absorbency by maximizing surface area. BIRD'S EYE, for example, consists of cotton or linen fibers

twisted loosely and then woven in a geometric or "dobby" pattern—in this case, with a small dot or "bird's eye" in each tiny square. CRASH is a rough weave of thick, uneven yarns; CRASH LINEN refers to a blend of linen, cotton, and rayon that proved highly effective in drying dishes because the rayon, derived from wood pulp, speeded up evaporation. DAMASK more often describes cloth used for tables, but the same jacquard pattern, firm body, and smooth, almost glossy finish can make a fine lint-free dish towel. HUCK towels combine thick yarns in a dobby weave, resulting in a textured honeycomb that looks and feels like little seeds. See the embroidered initial hand towel on page 26, for example. Huck cloth, sometimes called huckaback, lends itself to "Swedish embroidery" or "huck weaving"—a decorative threading technique that weaves embroidery threads just under the top fibers, so that the design isn't visible from the back of the cloth. TERRY, probably the most absorbent of all weaves, makes for a great hand towel because the cotton warp is allowed to loop on one or both sides, quadrupling surface area. TWILL, a woven fabric characterized by its diagonal pattern, can be used for toweling, but the tighter the weave, the more water-*resistant* it becomes. WAFFLE WEAVE, the result of using double-stranded yarns, makes for thirsty hand towels, but the cloth can shrink quite a bit and curl at the edges.

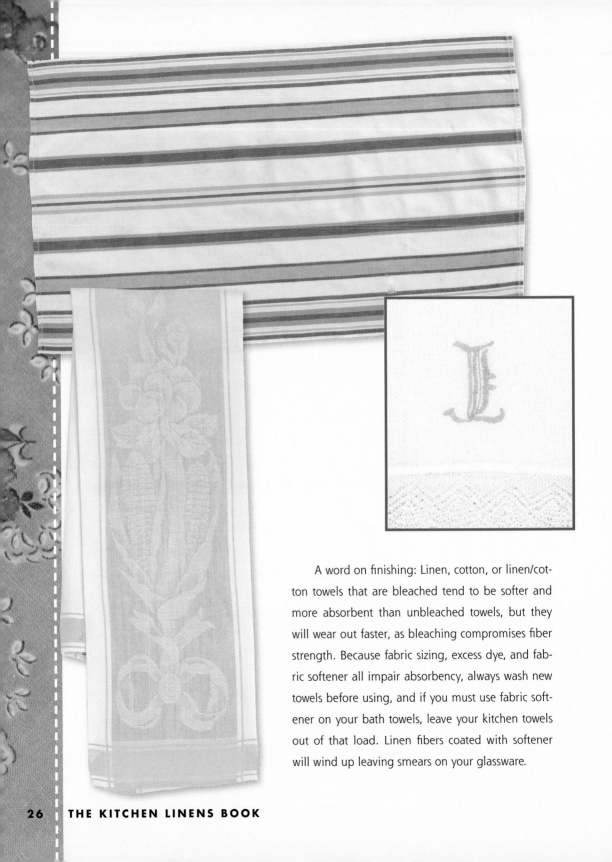

A word on finishing: Linen, cotton, or linen/cotton towels that are bleached tend to be softer and more absorbent than unbleached towels, but they will wear out faster, as bleaching compromises fiber strength. Because fabric sizing, excess dye, and fabric softener all impair absorbency, always wash new towels before using, and if you must use fabric softener on your bath towels, leave your kitchen towels out of that load. Linen fibers coated with softener will wind up leaving smears on your glassware.

# Carlyn Berghoff

*I*n most families, kids learn to tie their first bow on a shoe, with shoe-laces, on a box with a ribbon wrapped around it, or around two fingers (held up by some patient grown-up) with a piece of string. I learned to tie my first bow on an apron—my mother's. I belong to a restaurant family, and when we weren't in the restaurant (the Berghoff in Chicago), we were in the kitchen cooking, or around the table eating.

One morning when I was five years old, I stood behind my mother at the stove, where she was cooking eggs, and practiced making a bow on her apron. After I had made what I considered a successful bow, I went to the counter and started slicing up an apple for the fruit bowl. I not only cut the apple, but my finger as well. "Go to the powder room and run cold water over it, honey," said my mother, distractedly. "I'll be right there."

By the time she got there, I had fainted. And what a grand experience that turned out to be! She put me in bed, bandaged my little cut, and then brought me breakfast on a "sick tray." It was a hinged tray with supports on each side so that it fit over your legs as you sat up in bed. My mother put a white linen napkin on it, and a little vase with fresh flowers. And of course there was my breakfast, on pretty dishes with silverware on each side. It was a breakfast fit for a queen.

**MOST OF** my kitchen linens come from the postwar period, which was a time of both tremendous prosperity and industry. GIs and their brides moved into new homes and filled them with modern conveniences and appliances. It was definitely the heyday of the homemaker and the sewing machine. I have some *Good Housekeeping* and *House Beautiful* issues from this period and they are just brimming with DIY (do-it-yourself) projects: slipcovers, vanity table drapes, travel bags, window shades, house dresses and children's rompers, embroidery for hand towels, cozies to keep biscuits warm, and even covers for the toaster and mixer. Transfers, or line drawings you could iron onto fabric for embroidering, were still quite popular.

*RINSE AND SOAK dishes if you do not have time to wash them as soon as the meal is over. Soak oil or sugar-crusted pans in hot water; use cold water to soak pans that have had eggs, flour, or milk in them.*

## COVER IT!

Vintage appliance covers were an inexpensive way of dressing up a kitchen. The "Hot Toast Makes The . . . ," with the butterfly rebus, is an embroidered toaster cover that I discovered in a dusty bin at an antique store. I couldn't believe the original tag was still attached. What a find!

The sewing frenzy of the '50s extended beyond decorative coverings for appliances to cozies for bread goods—biscuits, muffins, and rolls—as a means of retaining their fresh-from-the-oven warmth. What amazes me about these creations is how small they are, hardly the size of a dinner plate today. Clearly our muffins are twice as big as they were fifty years ago! I love the way these cozies are tiered. You pull up on the center loop and all the little biscuit caves are apparent. The one made of Belgian lace comes up like a 3-D card to reveal six pockets. I can't see that buns would stay warm in such a thing, but it is charming (and perfectly sized to hold earrings and rings!). The only truly practical one is the large muslin cozy edged in green bias tape: A small bowl would fit inside, making it a casserole cover or carrier, too.

HOT TOAST
MAKES THE

Toaster Cover
For Easy-To-Do
Embroidery

HOT TOAST

Walker's
Transfer Pattern

CLOTHS•SCARFS
LINENS

# Dish Washing
## RITUALS

*I*n our first home together, Hank and I lived in a three-room, unheated log cabin. The kitchen was a setup of bare-necessity appliances, except for a nonelectric plastic dishwasher we received as a wedding gift from Steve Weinstein, Hank's college roommate. Steve managed to choose the one present that truly transformed our lives at that point. The dishwasher sat sinkside and, when filled, was hooked up to the tap via a screw-on hose. Water pressure made a series of spritzers spew hot water over the dishes, all of it taking place under a plastic dome. Hank and I would stand there mesmerized, the same way you'd watch exotic fish in an aquarium.

Now, of course, I have a built-in dishwasher, one that is barely audible during any of its half-dozen wash-and-dry cycle options. My job is to load it, because I enjoy angling the sweetest little robin's egg blue scalloped-edge bowls between the bulbs of wineglasses, and a row of yellow vintage-ware cups with square handles in a line down the center. Hank will unload it, which suits me fine. If we've had a dinner party, I might leave a sink full of serving pieces and roasting pans to soak, and go to bed; I don't find rising Saturday or Sunday morning to face the mess difficult at all. But on weeknights, I finish the job no matter how pooped I might be because I do not, absolutely not, want to begin the next morning seeing leftover anything from the night before.

In fact, my final act in setting the kitchen to rights is to drape a fresh dish towel over whatever I've washed the night before as it air-dries on the counter or dish rack. The pretty towel is the first thing I see in the morning, and it just brightens my spirit. This act of draping is something I learned from my Grandma Manya. She had a pet parakeet and, at night, she sang to it in Russian while settling a bright cloth over its cage. Upon awakening, she entered the kitchen, slowly rolled back the cloth, and greeted the bird in her native language. This grandmother was the gentlest person in my world, and I adored her. Like a kind word or a sweet coo, a pretty cloth is a beautiful beginning to any person's—or any bird's—day.

## from the linen closet
### *Jan Smallwood*

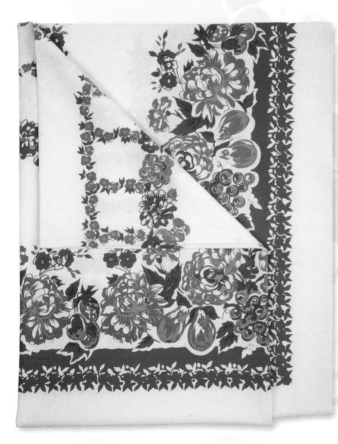

This cloth belonged to my mother-in-law, Mona Gae Presley Smallwood. Her father was a first or second cousin to Vernon Presley, Elvis's father. She lived a rural life in Southern Ohio. Her cloths, like everything she put into the home, were her worldly goods and her personal wealth. Because of their importance to her, all the household's linens were saved. They are precious heirlooms now, and I am safeguarding them for my daughters and my granddaughter.

DESIGNS THAT showcased the conveniences of a modern kitchen and other aspects of the good life characterized cloths from the '50s. One of my favorites is a jumbo piece called "Kitchen Parade" made by Startex and offered by Montgomery Ward catalogs in 1956. It was sold as a dish towel but, at thirty inches square, could easily be a small table-cloth. You could double- or quadruple-fold it and get a lot of mileage out of it between washings, or make curtains, which the manufacturer encouraged.

**I SUSPECT** that my Mexican-themed luncheon cloth is also from the '50s. I love the primary colors of this one, and its pottery motif. At the time, Mexico represented a very exciting destination. Acapulco then had the cachet of, say, Havana and the Tropicana nightclub. Maybe that's why these south-of-the-border kitchen linens and souvenir aprons are in such great condition: They weren't purchased to use. Rather, they were purchased as reminders of the trip and something to show the neighbors along with the vacation snapshots. I like using souvenir cloths and aprons because I enjoy their vibrancy and find them historically interesting.

part two

# GATHERING AND GABBING

*"I can just imagine myself sitting down at the head of
the table and pouring out the tea," said Anne, shutting
her eyes ecstatically. "And asking Diana if she takes
sugar! I know she doesn't but of course I'll ask her just as
if I didn't know. And then pressing her to take another
piece of fruit cake and another helping of preserves."*

—*Anne of Green Gables*, Lucy Maud Montgomery

**WE'RE NOT** entertaining the way we used to.

Have you noticed? We meet at a coffee shop after dropping off children or coming from the gym. Or we arrange "to do lunch" and meet at a restaurant. Or you and your partner, or a date, are invited to come to dinner . . . which turns out to be Chinese takeout.

We're interacting and entertaining a lot less formally than our mothers and grandmothers did. But as long as the focus remains on getting together with friends to sit, eat, and chat, that's okay. Being a great hostess is about making your guests feel you've made time for them—and issuing the invitation in the first place.

Personally, I'm a great fan of smaller gatherings: one or two friends, certainly no more than five. It can be for lunch, or a late-afternoon cup of tea before everyone has to rush home to start dinner. It can be soup and a salad, or just a fabulous dessert. The beauty of these little daytime gatherings in my home is the opportunity they give me to provide my friends with a bit of respite from the hectic pace of their day. I enjoy creating a special ambience for just a few, something not always so easily accomplished when dealing with a crowd. And the

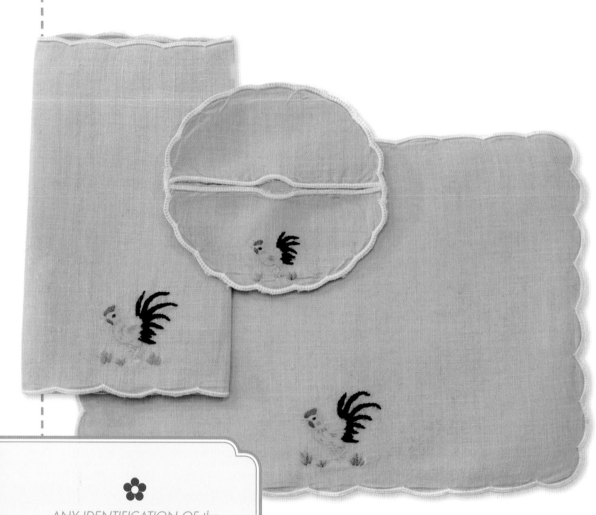

time frame needn't cut into anybody's day: forty-five minutes to an hour and a half, tops. Women have jobs to get back to, in and out of the home. That's why forty-five minutes of pure relaxation during the day is such a welcome treat.

For tables that enchant, I'll pull out my prettiest cloths and daintiest napkins. To me, what makes a linen perfect for a luncheon is not the size of the cloth but rather how feminine or

delicate it is. Pink brocade, rows of twining roses,
hand-done hemstitch or cutwork, embroidered bouquets
of flowers, and embellishments like rickrack inspire my choices.
If I have an apron of the same vintage, then that decides it. Women invariably ooh and
aah over the intricacy of a monogram or the fineness of a linen, and they know how to
use a tiny napkin. (My turquoise linen napkins, for example, may have been intended
for the cocktail hour, but at 5"×7¼", they're perfect for tea with my girlfriends.) And
who else would appreciate crocheted doilies as table decorations or as a covering to a
cup or glass?

Among the most feminine of my finds is an untouched tea set of Portuguese or Madeira linen. I know it's never been used because the napkins are still tacked together and the paper tags are still affixed. Looking at the little tufts of lace tucked into the scalloped edge of the cloth, I marvel how someone just let this set go without a second thought as to how it might pretty-up a tray or vanity. True, the napkins are tiny and dainty, and the cloth would barely cover a card table, but I'll be layering it over a larger cloth anyway, to emphasize the work along the edge and corners. For a centerpiece I might use the Limoges box my dear friend Marilyn Wilson gave me, which normally sits in my writing room so that I can admire it every day. And for my apron I'd choose this batiste beauty from the '20s, whose fine embroidery and silk ribbon straps transform the lawn dress I'm inclined to wear for summertime luncheons.

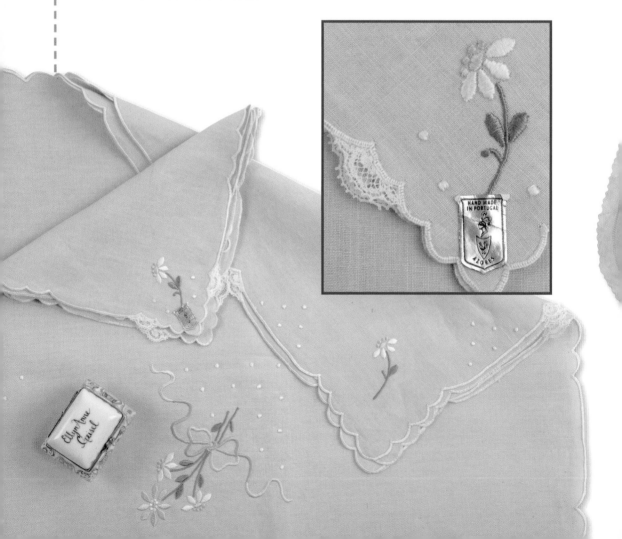

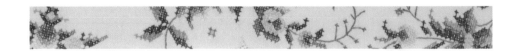

## from the linen closet
## *Loretta Madden*

$\mathcal{M}$y sister Lorraine and I earned our college tuition by working in our small mountain town's restaurant. It was a hectic place to work, since not only did the town swell to four times its yearly population during the summer months, but we also fed the college students staying in town for a geological field camp. To feed those students before they headed out for the day, we were expected to be at the restaurant by 5:30 a.m. Then we tended to the regular customers for breakfast, lunch, and dinner. In between shifts, we made the sack lunches for the students, washed the dishes, tossed salads, peeled potatoes, and cleaned the cabins.

Bertie Skrifvars, the owner of the restaurant, worked right alongside us. She was the cook and, with all the responsibility on her, she'd lash out at us sometimes with some pretty harsh words. The next day, it was as if those words had never been spoken.

Then came the summer we graduated from college and no longer needed to work for Bertie. She presented each of us with a beautifully crocheted tablecloth, large enough to cover a rectangular table with all the leaves put in. She told us that every time she took a stitch, she thought of the awful words she had said and how thankful she was that we forgave her by coming back to work every morning. Her fatigue and frustration were aimed not at us, but at her circumstances at that moment.

The ecru tablecloths, crocheted in cotton in a series of small circular shapes, are over forty years old now. I bring mine out for very special occasions and lay it over several colored cloths. It's a reminder of

Bertie's faith in us, and her joy
that we became teachers and escaped
a life of manual labor. We had, as Bertie would say, "done
her proud."

## DECORATIVE TECHNIQUES

The world's oldest fabric decoration, EMBROIDERY refers to the art of making stitched designs and patterns in fabric using a needle. CROSS-STITCH is any embroidery that involves the counting of threads in the ground material and the use of X (cross) -shaped stitches. APPLIQUÉ is needlework in which pieces of fabric or lace are sewn onto a ground fabric to form decorative designs. OPENWORK refers to fabric ornamented by pulling threads, cutting fabric away after embroidering, or a lace that is attached to a foundation fabric. DRAWNWORK means that threads are literally drawn out of the weave and the remaining threads are grouped and stitched together leaving an opening. The first laces

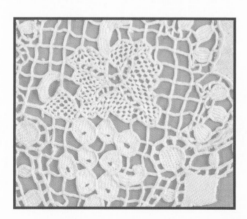

originated this way. When threads were cut or drawn away, creating a grid of open spaces, the technique was called RETICELLA. PUNTO IN ARIA is distinguished from reticella, because it is stitched "in air" rather than on the actual fabric; after it is completed, the design is attached to the ground fabric. CUTWORK is woven fabric from which threads have been cut away with sharp scissors or a razor to form intricate patterns; the openings in cutwork are usually outlined with closely spaced stitches like those used to finish buttonholes, and may be embellished with white embroidery. Similar to cutwork, EYELET is fabric in which small holes are cut in round, oval, or tear shapes.

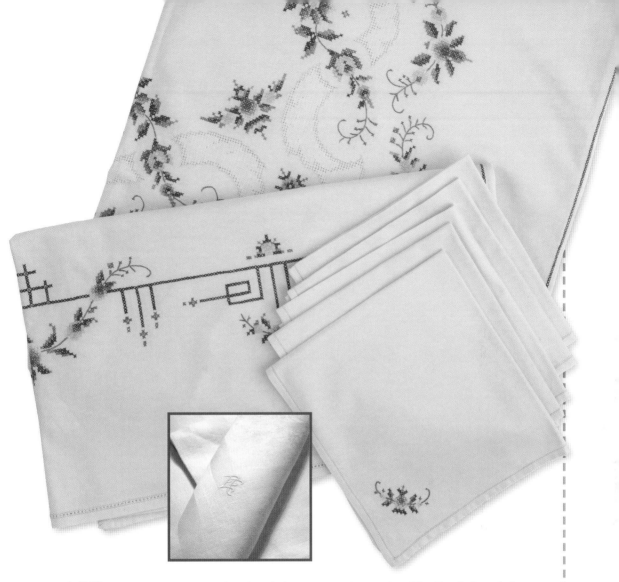

**I DID** inherit some exquisite handwork from my mother-in-law, Else Frank Geisel. As a young woman, she had been apprenticed to a couture shop in London. She once told me her expertise as a seamstress there was hand-bound buttonholes, which explains the exactness of the embroidery on a dozen damask napkins. Embroidered during World War II, these napkins bearing her maiden initials accompanied her to America in 1946. When I use them, I think of Else all alone in London, in despair about her family's fate in Germany, and yet still hopeful for a future where she would set a beautiful table. An intricately cross-stitched cloth was among the collection we discovered when Hank and I cleaned out her apartment. The cloth is large enough to seat eight, but I set it for fewer guests so that the

embroidery can be seen as an expanse and really appreciated. Likewise, a cloth I have from the '40s or '50s deserves to be admired in all its crocheted glory: The blue edge was added as a finishing touch, and the work is so exacting you'd think it was done by machine. When I use this cloth, I wear this organza apron because the little crocheted edge on the pockets draws even more attention to the cloth.

Handwork always catches my eye, and not because it raises the value of the linen (although of course it does): You just have to realize that there are hundreds of stitches per square inch in some of the finer examples. I have lovely green-bordered napkins with what appears to me to be reticella, a form of cutwork where threads were taken out of the weave

to form a grid of square holes and then reintroduced to fill that grid with a pattern. I like to pair them with my St. Regis red geranium tablecloth, circa 1940s, because the greens in both have been washed to the same fade and softness.

Much of the handwork I admire went into monograms on napkins. I find them to be little works of art, really—especially this one rendered on, quite unfortunately, a flimsy weave of cotton that is falling apart. Front and back, the stitches are perfect; there isn't a fray or visible knot. Such attention to detail, and all just to pretty-up a dish towel! Despite the fabric's deterioration, I like to feature it by putting it on a

## from the linen closet
### Abigail Foulk

My mother, Joanne, is a wonderful gift-giver. She has a special knack for knowing what a person will enjoy and appreciate—and she is famous for giving tablecloths, April Cornell's designs being her favorite. So for her eightieth birthday, we knew a great celebration was in order, one involving not just children and grandchildren but high school friends, college roommates, camp friends, and co-workers. And on the invitation we sent out we made one request: bring any and all tablecloths you've received as gifts from Joanne.

The party was held at the Montshire Museum in Norwich, Vermont. I will never forget the look of surprise and joy on Mom's face when she arrived at her birthday celebration to find these two hundred guests seated at tables adorned with colorful and vibrant tablecloths of her own choosing.

We also set up a clothesline at the party to display artifacts and memorabilia from Mom's life. There were favorite trinkets from childhood and a letter she had received from her father at summer camp. But the grand spectacle, the crème de la crème, the pièce de résistance that had everyone congregating at the clotheslines were the monogrammed hand towels, napkins, runners, and tablecloths—Joanne's vintage linens blowing in the Vermont breeze.

platter or tray, folding it so you can't see anything but the monogram. The towel is over eighty years old, after all, and its embroidery deserves to be admired for years to come. The fact that the three initials are not my own isn't important to me; displaying her artistry is.

I do have one pink hand towel with my own initial on it—not for lack of looking! (The EL napkin and the ELB fingertip towel are wedding presents my friend Julie Johnson discovered at a rummage store. An amazing bit of thrifting luck, the initials are identical to her cousin's maiden and married names.) Regardless of initial, I collect monogrammed napkins—place mats, too—because so much ingenuity and self-expression went into their design. I can't always tell just what the letters are. For the longest time I stared at my set of six embroidered napkins from the 1920s, turning them this way and that, trying to figure out what the initial was. Out of the blue one day, I saw that it wasn't one letter, but two: a D inside an L! Originally, I'm told, monograms were created to identify linens that were sent out for cleaning—in much the same way you'd write your child's name on all his clothes before he went off to camp. Another explanation is that the status of women in the Victorian age precluded them from owning property, except for household goods or "paraphernalia," which included silver. To prove ownership, women engraved the goods with their maiden initials, which they then passed on to their daughters. Good for them. I love the result.

Above all, with my friends I like to mix things up to keep the mood fun rather than formal. I'll put a lively 1930s flour-sack runner on top of a cloth whose center is stained or in need of a centerpiece. I might use one of my Depression-era aprons on top of a faded breakfast cloth for a shabby-chic effect. I've got a cloth whose palette of orange-gold and green doesn't thrill me, but whose erratic embroidery comes alive when paired with a dresser scarf of the same color combination. I'd place the runner so the crocheted skirt meets up with the aster border. And I wouldn't hesitate to bring out my collection of Tupperware iced-tea spoons, to pick up the pastel shades in the embroidery of a round cloth distinguished by cutwork and lace. Why ever not?

In that same eclectic spirit, I'd feature what I think of as my Alice Kramden cloth. It's not even cloth but a heavy plastic, pliable and cloudy, unlike anything you'd find today. Its edges are hemmed on all four sides and printed with a red, yellow, and blue plaid that frames individual flowers. I got very excited when I saw it, because it dates back to the '50s and was still in the original packaging. My first thought, when I laid eyes on it, was Alice from *The Honeymooners*, because she would have delighted in its convenience. Harriet Nelson would not have gone gaga over this plastic cloth. Harriet would have insisted on cotton gingham; but for Alice, who lived in an apartment building where the washing machine was down in the basement, a table covering you could wipe down with a sponge would have been a godsend.

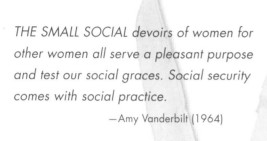

The Alice cloth inspires me to throw a retro luncheon for a few of my working friends. I've got a printed plastic apron to wear and bright patterned napkins to pick up on the colors in the cloth. The whole ensemble begs for mismatched plates and those little juice glasses that jelly used to come in. I'm going to serve a basil tomato soup and a platter of egg-salad sandwiches on toast points. If it were summertime, I'd be tempted to mix up a blender of chocolate malted milk shakes, like my mother used to do, and put out a bowl of seasoned oyster crackers or potato chips to munch on.

In the powder room, I look to provide the necessities in unexpected ways. I feature my linens, first and foremost: delicately finished finger towels, embroidered hand towels, cocktail napkins with charming appliqué, even dish towels that are too ornamental for kitchen duty. I hang them on a towel rack from those little clips one uses to hang curtains from a rod. And just to eliminate that confusion about whether these little beauties are really to be used, I hang them a tad off kilter, or I slightly wrinkle or dampen one. If the towels are napkins, I do a show-and-tell, leaving out a little basket with a rumpled one already tossed in.

Likewise, I'll layer little hotel and figurine soaps in a crystal ashtray and wash my hands with the top one so my guests don't hesitate to. (I hate being confounded by gorgeous bowls full of pristine shaped and scented little soaps that have clearly never been touched—are they for me to use or what?) I've put guest soaps in a silver gravy boat, to get use from it other than on Thanksgiving. And lately I've been putting out items for my guests that I always wish I might encounter when freshening up at other people's houses: dental floss, breath mints, and hand lotion, all set on a pretty doily in a tray or serving dish or an old tin lunch box. To me, it's all about accommodating and delighting myself along with my friends.

To get the party rolling, consider whom to invite. Don't agonize over this. Think of women you haven't seen in a while, friends you'd really like to catch up with or someone new you'd like to know better. Even just one friend. And whether by e-mail, snail mail, or telephone, invite her to join you on a specific day and time.

*Dear Terrie,*

*It's been ages since just the two of us sat and visited. If you're available next Thursday at twelve thirty for an hour or so, I'll fix a bit of lunch and we can catch up.*

Just like that. Simple!

## QUICHE LORRAINE

1 9-inch frozen pie crust,
    defrosted
8 slices cooked and crumbled
    bacon (packaged,
    precooked bacon works
    just fine)
2 cups shredded Swiss cheese
¼ cup chopped onion
4 eggs

½ cup sour cream
½ cup milk or half-and-half
1 teaspoon dry mustard
Pinch of nutmeg

Preheat the oven to 425°F. Sprinkle the bacon, cheese, and onion on the bottom of the unbaked pie crust.

In a bowl or blender, beat the eggs, then add the remaining ingredients and beat to combine. Pour this egg mixture into the pie shell.

Bake at 425°F for 15 minutes. Reduce temperature to 325°F; continue to bake for 30 to 40 minutes or until a knife inserted near the center comes out clean. Let stand 10 minutes before cutting.

**NOW, WHAT** are you going to serve?

Stick with your druthers. What would you make for yourself? I happen to love bacon; one of the rituals I share with my sister Carol is making a towering BLT, the layers slathered with real mayonnaise, and each of us eating half. For a guest, though, I'd turn the BLT into a salad of romaine lettuce, chopped plum tomatoes, shredded hardboiled egg, slices of avocado, bacon crumbles, and a creamy dressing, served with warm-from-the-oven crescent rolls and pats of genuine butter on the side. (For individual finger servings, halve the plum tomatoes lengthwise. Scoop out the insides and fill the halves with a mixture of cooked and crumbled bacon, mayo, and chopped green onion. Sprinkle

### VARIATIONS:

- Replace 1 cup Swiss with sharp Cheddar or Gruyère.
- Substitute ham or cooked sweet Italian sausage for the bacon.
- Add diced green chiles, or asparagus and mushrooms; be sure to drain canned goods.
- Add diced fresh tomatoes, first pressing between paper towels to remove excess liquid.

### CRUST VARIATION:

Preheat the oven to 425°F. Thaw 3 cups frozen hash browns and squeeze between paper towels to "dry." Press into the bottom and up the sides of a greased 9-inch pie plate. Drizzle with 5⅓ tablespoons of melted butter and bake at 425°F for 25 minutes. Prepare the filling and bake as above.

with Parmesan and broil 10 minutes or until the tomatoes start to wilt.)

Quiche is a hugely versatile dish, one you can bake ahead or put together at the last minute, and one you can eat for brunch, lunch, or dinner, either cold, room temperature, or hot out of the oven. The key is to have premade shells in your freezer or a box of rolled-up Pillsbury pie crusts in the fridge. If you've got eggs and cheese—and most of us do, at any given moment—then it's a cinch to blend them in advance; cook the bacon and chop the onion ahead, too, so that all can be combined at the last minute and baked. A savory quiche right out of the oven served with a green salad is my no-fail recipe for an easy-to-prepare sit-down with a friend.

## CHOCOLATE MOUSSE

¼ cup sugar

3 tablespoons rum

¼ pound semisweet chocolate

2 egg whites (yolks are not used)

2 tablespoons whipping (double) cream

2 cups whipped cream

In a small pot, heat the sugar and rum over very low heat, stirring until the sugar is dissolved.

Melt the chocolate in a double boiler or microwave oven, then stir in the 2 tablespoons of whipping cream. Add the sugar mixture and stir until smooth. Allow to cool (don't chill in the refrigerator).

Beat the egg whites until stiff. Fold into the cooled chocolate mixture, then gently fold this mixture into the whipped cream. Portion into 4 to 6 sherbet glasses (or leave in the bowl) and chill in the refrigerator at least 2 hours before serving.

A word about dessert: You'll need to buy or make one. I happen to feel strongly about this. To my way of thinking, dessert is the reason to eat a healthy meal. When my boys were little I'd show them the cake I'd made as they sat down to dinner, just so they'd have the right incentive. Friends of ours still kid me about the time they brought out fresh fruit for dessert and I, hugely pregnant and craving a chocolate ending to the meal, burst into tears. Fruit is not dessert. Chocolate mousse is dessert. Banana pudding, my signature dessert dish, is something I could make and serve every day and never tire of it. Cake of any kind is dessert. Frosted cupcakes decorated with plastic cupcake picks—like the pink elephants and blue ducks and green roosters that I found at a flea market—are dessert.

# How to
## Brew a Proper Pot of Tea

Order a cup of tea in a restaurant, and you'll be presented with an assortment of tea bags and a little pot of hot water. This is not "serving" tea, though. The only real cup of tea is one that has been properly brewed.

The correct brew comes from tea leaves that are allowed to fully expand in a preheated teapot filled with water that has been boiled in a separate kettle. Should you be so lucky as to own a sterling service, this is the time to show it off. An ironstone, china, or ceramic teapot is just fine, however. Whatever you use, be sure you "hot the pot" with a dose of boiling water first, for about a minute. Dump that out and spoon in loose tea directly or use a tea-leaf basket. Measure carefully: Usually the ratio is about one teaspoon of dry leaves per six-ounce cup. Use water that is boiling— anything less and the results will be mediocre. And time the brew: Tea needs to steep, usually from four to six minutes, but no more, because overbrewing is as ruinous to the flavor as underbrewing. Pour the tea through a strainer to remove the tea leaves (hence the advantage of using a tea basket). Cover the pot of brewed tea with a cozy to keep it piping hot.

My favorite cake is coconut and the best one I've tasted is a recipe hailing from Birmingham. Basically you make a four-layer cake from a box of white cake mix, then mix up a filling/icing of 2 cups of sour cream, 2 cups of sugar, and 18 ounces of coconut. Set aside 1¼ cup of this, and spread the rest between the layers. Add 1½ cups of whipped topping to the reserved mixture, and use this to ice the cake. Then cover the cake with plastic wrap (first studding the top and sides with toothpicks, to keep the wrap off the icing), and refrigerate it for four days. Who knows if this amount of mellowing is really necessary, but I follow these directions every time and it always turns out to be the moistest, most delicious cake.

I may serve dessert alone, without the meal. The English call this afternoon tea, and, given my feelings about dessert, I think this is a perfectly wonderful way to entertain friends. Hot tea as a hospitality beverage was not in my repertoire until I visited London. Hank and I had been sightseeing and shopping all afternoon, and what with the jet lag, by four o'clock we were in desperate need of a pick-me-up. We called a halt to currency conversion and sought respite in a tearoom.

Seated at a pristine white cloth–covered table, we ordered the traditional tea menu—a pot of hot Darjeeling and assorted "biscuits," cakes, and savories. In quick succession, the waitress delivered a three-tiered silver server of dainty sandwiches; sliced fruits and delightful pastries; and a china teapot wearing what looked to me like a small quilted bathrobe.

Whether it was the elegance of our surroundings, the indulgence of a late afternoon tryst with my Prince Charming, or the civility of sipping an aromatic beverage poured from a lovely china pot dressed in a cozy, I tossed aside my preference for pitchers of sweet, iced tea in favor of this gracious combination of hot tea and dessert.

It was Anna Maria, the Duchess of Bedford and lady-in-waiting to Queen Victoria, who is credited with inventing afternoon tea, by the way. She took to nibbling sweets with her cup of brew to quell those midafternoon stomach rumblings. Soon the queen was taking her tea with munchies, too. With that royal stamp of approval, tea became a daily afternoon entertaining opportunity for the Victorian hostess both in England and America.

## Tea Menu Ideas

*Finger sandwiches made on crustless bread triangles*

*Miniature biscuits, croissants, or scones*

*Quiche*

*Seasonal fruit salad*

*Petits fours*

*Tartlets*

*Cream puffs*

*Assorted chocolates*

*Cookies*

**PROPER TEA** preparation is so rich with ritual, it can be the very reason to have a tea party. Still, for tea with a friend or two, I pare the ceremony to the basics and brew tea in beautiful china cups, filling vintage strainers with tea leaves and pouring water from a decorative pot. I have a sterling silver set I adore, not just for its heft but also for its grace. I love the round bellies of the sugar bowl and creamer; each and every piece sits on four darling little feet. You can't beat sterling for holding heat or, for that matter, keeping things cold.

There are a host of implements to accompany serving tea: tongs, for sugar cubes; a silver tea strainer, with its own table coaster; a stunning variety of tea baskets, filters, mesh balls, paper sachets, perforated spoons, and infusers; and teaspoons, identifiable by their size or ornament. But best of all, for my money, are the cozies: They inspire all manner of artistry. See my friend Gloria Kirchhoff's Sock Monkey on the opposite page, for example.

*HOSTING A TEA party is appropriate any afternoon, for any reason. Time-wise, aim for after 3:00 p.m. but before 5:00 p.m., lest it interfere with dinner or evening plans.*

Whether I serve tea and cookies or coffee and cake or even hot chocolate and popcorn, I've come to see the late-afternoon get-together as a near-perfect time to gather with my girlfriends. We all sit, and nibble, and chat—my three most favorite things. Relaxing in one another's company, we visit in a way that just doesn't happen when men are around. And my friends won't need to rush off, because I'm sending them home with dinner. While we're talking pedal-to-the-metal in the living room, I've got quiches baking in the oven. When the timer goes off, I know it's time to pull out those pies, wrap them in a pretty dish towel, and present them to my guests. Because there is nothing nicer we can do for each other, I think, than solving the whole what's-for-dinner question, if only for one night.

## from the linen closet
### Judy Foreman

*B*eing a stepparent is not the easiest job, but Marshall, whom my mother married after divorcing my father, made it his business to try and be the best stepdad there ever was. Nothing made him happier than when I called him Dad, as I was the daughter he never had. That acknowledgment meant more to him than any Father's Day card or birthday gift.

For forty years, he was always the first one there when I had a problem or needed help. An architect, he assisted me in remodeling four homes and attended my kids' soccer, basketball, volleyball games, graduations, and theatrical performances. His

only failure was trying to teach me mathematics and his only frustration was not marrying me off for good. He hated that I lived alone after my divorce, even though I told him I was happy. It just never sat right with him.

Ever one to think and behave "outside the box," Marshall one year asked my mom, who was a whiz with all things involving needles, to teach him cross-stitching. I think he genuinely liked the work, being rather artistic and a terrific painter. But I suspect he also liked the idea of a big guy like himself doing delicate stitchery. He decided to embroider an entire tablecloth for me as an anniversary gift. For months, he took it with him when he traveled, and many a stewardess wondered who this man was, doing ladies' work. A giant oval with pink and green stitching in a floral pattern, the tablecloth apparently reminded him of his grandmother, whom he lived with after his mother died when he was twelve. She always had good linen at her Jewish holiday dinners on the West Side of Chicago. I've loved setting my own holiday table with Marshall's cloth, and now it is my greatest treasure.

# part three

# PICNICS AND TAILGATES

*"I wanted to tell you about the pic-nic."*

*"O, that's jolly. Who's going to give it?"*

*"My ma's going to let me have one."*

*"O, goody; I hope she'll let me come."*

*"Well she will. The pic-nic's for me. She'll let anybody come that I want, and I want you."*

—Becky Thatcher and Tom Sawyer, Mark Twain's *The Adventures of Tom Sawyer*

**WHEN HANK** and I were living in Boulder, we used to drive up to Gold Hill, an old mining camp northwest of town that you could only get to by dirt roads. We'd park and walk in a bit to the middle of this field of tall grass and then plop down on our quilt and take in the view. We loved to go in the fall, not only to look at the changing aspens, but to listen to them. When the wind stirred the leaves you could hear this tinkling sound, like an orchestra of wind chimes. Just to lie there and look out at the leaves flashing in the sun was enough, really. But even romance needs sustenance, so we'd take a picnic.

I wasn't much of a cook in those days; we'd have stopped at City Market, which was kind of like Whole Foods before there ever was a Whole Foods, and picked up what in our minds was very Parisian repast: some Brie cheese, a baguette, a cluster of grapes, and a bottle of Mateus. We'd carry it all into the field in our backpacks, not because we were mountaineers but because hiking gear was the look of living in Boulder: lace-up boots, heavy socks, cutoff Levi's with frayed edges, and a layering of shirts, with the tie-dyed one last. (Ever the fashionista, I wore John Lennon sunglasses and dangly earrings.) And then we'd spread our quilt and settle in for the afternoon.

During a recent spate of seasonal cleaning, I opened an old suitcase and found our quilt inside. As I pulled it from its hiding place, I remembered packing it up for posterity some thirty-three years ago. The quilt doesn't look all that much the worse for wear, although you can see some moth damage and, in the threadbare spots, more of the blanket that lies under the patchwork. I'm sure I bought it in some local secondhand store, along with all our other furnishings. Even though it was pieced with fabric from somebody else's life, for somebody else's bed, it played to all my romantic notions, because I'd never had a handmade quilt in my whole life.

If I were to use it now for a picnic, I'd make it the foundation and then spread a red-and-white weave cloth on it, something with wide checks. That way you can pull up the corners of the cloth when you're done eating and move it and everything on it off the quilt, just like clearing a table. That would leave us a place to lie or sit and talk.

But since finding it, I must admit, I allow myself to daydream of a third purpose for this old quilt: of playing with a grandchild on it. I remember putting my own babies on a small quilted coverlet and watching them wiggle about on their bellies. They'd take their little pincher fingers and pluck at all the colors. The fabric on this one is all worn and soft, and in the middle of every four-square there's a knot of embroidery thread that'd be perfect for plucking at. For our grandbaby, I'd triple this quilt with others to make a good padded surface. Then Hank and I could lie there all comfy and cuddle, and watch our grandbaby play while its parents were off doing we know what in the hills.

# *Picnics*
## THROUGH HISTORY

*I*f you think about it, the earliest meal was of course a picnic—simple food prepared simply and eaten outside, with or without company. And as civilized as we've become, we've never outgrown our fondness for it. Everything seems to taste better outside, or maybe our appetite is just sharpened by fresh air. Picnics certainly seem simpler to prepare and clean up than meals made for indoor dining. Or it's the attitude we bring: At a picnic, we're focused more on socializing than eating, on the fun of food rather than the work of preparing it.

The word *picnic*, in fact, originally meant a meal made up of dishes that each guest brought—what today we'd call a potluck. It was a get-together without a host, making it a carefree event even if it didn't take place outdoors. But such gatherings often did, and so the word morphed in meaning from a potluck meal to a meal taken anywhere that wasn't home. The Victorians were particularly fond of picnics, maybe because it gave them a rare opportunity to socialize without all the formality. Jane Austen liked to send her characters out into the woods and fields to dine. One of the most famous images from the era is of a picnic: *Le Dejeuner sur l'Herbe*, Edouard Manet's huge canvas of gentlemen reclining in a forest glade on a cloth with baskets of fruit and a lady friend who happens not to be wearing anything. Other impressionists, including Renoir, Monet, and Cézanne, picked up on the picnic theme as well. (In Renoir's *Luncheon of the Boating Party*, it's the men who are half-dressed and the women who remain buttoned up.)

> **Picnic**, from the seventeenth-century French,
> *piquenique*: *picorer*, which means "to pick" and *nique*,
> which means "something of little value."

Today our picnics take place just about anywhere, from suburban yards to public parks, out of the backs of our cars and along the highway, in grassy fields, sandy beaches, alpine meadows, and atop rugged peaks. They're prepared at home or cobbled together en route or

> **SEPARATE PERISHABLE FROM** *nonperishable items in your picnic basket or cooler (or better yet, take two separate containers). Wrap meat and poultry in double-strength plastic bags, so as not to contaminate other foods with leaking juices, and store these perishables close to the icepacks.*

cooked on site. In fact, barbecuing and picnicking go hand in hand, just as they did in medieval times, when the hunt party would roast and eat whatever they'd bagged that day before they ever left the forest. Now, as then, the women usually do all the prep and cleanup while the men do the fire-tending and grilling. The meal isn't necessarily simple: Tailgate picnics these days are notoriously complex, with hosts lugging gas grills, lounge furniture, televisions and stereos, and a generator to run it all. But the picnic spirit prevails. Whatever you call it—picnicking or barbecuing or tailgating—and whatever you make it—bread, cheese, and wine on a blanket or a five-course meal on table and chairs—it's still more about the company than the food, about the novelty of eating outdoors rather than the ritual of dining in. It's a state of mind, really. And we're looking to cultivate it wherever and whenever we can.

**AT ONE** time in my life, a tailgate was an outdoor family picnic. Summertime car trips always involved one, as we were a large family and dining at a restaurant was not an option. Halfway to our grandparents' home in Charleston, South Carolina, my mother would direct Daddy to stop at a roadside table. We'd pile out, she'd spread a cloth, and Daddy would haul from the back of the station wagon the baskets of food she'd prepared, along with a box of newspaper-wrapped milk bottles filled with water still slushy with melting ice. The baskets held foods we knew well: bologna sandwiches, fried chicken, potato chips, sliced sweet pickles, celery and carrot sticks, apples, grapes, bananas, and Oreos. Yet eating them at a wooden picnic table by the side of the highway on a weekday with our parents squished among us, we felt a gaiety and ticklish excitement.

After overnighting at my grandparents', we'd go to Tybee Beach. This meant driving down to Wilmington Island and having lunch at Aunt Mimi's with her brood and a throng of regional family. Living the farthest away, we were the excuse for a mini-reunion. Aunt Bobbie, Uncle Merrill, and the boy cousins plus Aunt Francis, Uncle Reuben, the girl cousins, and Aunt Rehette and Uncle Lukie would all assemble. The front of Aunt Mimi's house faced the water; the tailgate took place in the large backyard. I can remember the baskets coming out of the car, now filled with Grandma Birdye's homemade yeast breads, cinnamon rolls, fruit pies, the most delicious oatmeal-pecan cookies (see page 76), and bags of peaches and boiled peanuts purchased at roadside stands along the way. We'd eat under massive live oaks dripping with hanging moss, the grown-ups sitting at patio tables set with cloth and china while we kids sat cross-legged on beach rugs.

## The Beach Rug

With cotton terry on one side and a waterproof vinyl on the other, the beach rug doubles as a towel and a picnic cloth. You can make one easily enough by sewing a beach towel to oilcloth that's been cut to size—or even using Velcro to attach the two.

*TO REMOVE BEACH sand from your skin, sprinkle on baby powder. The sand slides right off.*

## GRANDMA BIRDYE'S OATMEAL-PECAN COOKIES

1 cup shortening

1 cup packed brown sugar

1 cup granulated sugar

2 eggs

1 teaspoon vanilla extract

1½ cups all-purpose flour

1 teaspoon baking soda

1 teaspoon salt

3 cups old-fashioned oats

1 cup chopped pecans

Preheat the oven to 350°F. Grease two baking sheets.

In a mixing bowl, cream the shortening and sugars. Add the eggs and vanilla. Combine the flour, baking soda, and salt separately; stir in gradually to the creamed mixture. Stir in the oats and nuts. Chill for 30 minutes.

Drop the dough by the tablespoon onto the prepared baking sheets, about 2 inches apart (or form into smallish balls, pressing just a bit to flatten). Bake at 350°F for 10 to 12 minutes, or until golden. Cool the cookies on wire racks.

Store in a cookie jar.

On another trip, we'd visit Aunt Beth, Uncle William, and two more cousins over in Beaufort, South Carolina. Picnics there came straight from their dock to the table; this was the low country, where crab and shrimp were caught, cooked, peeled, and picked clean in the screened-in kitchen dockside. Only the oysters came from

## COUSIN ANN KENNEDY'S
## DOCK PARTY CRAB PIE

2 cups fresh crab

1 cup shredded extra-sharp Cheddar

8 ounces cream cheese, cut into 1/2-inch cubes

½ cup sliced green onions

2 cups milk

1 cup Bisquick

4 eggs

¾ teaspoon salt

Preheat the oven to 400°F. Grease two pie plates.

In a bowl, stir together the crab, Cheddar, cream cheese, and green onions. Divide the mixture between the two prepared pie plates.

Place the remaining ingredients in a blender and blend on a low to medium speed for 1 minute.

Pour the blender contents over crab mixture in the pie plates. Bake at 400°F for about 30 minutes. Let stand for 5 minutes before serving.

elsewhere, purchased from "the oyster people" because their beds were trustworthy. I can remember watching the adults bring up huge pots of steaming shellfish and boiled ears of corn to the lawn, where boards were set up as a waist-high table. There they'd dump the seafood and corn in bowls. Sticks of butter and little bowls of dipping sauce were within everyone's reach, and it was a free-for-all of rolling and dipping and eating with our fingers. The grown-ups wore huge napkins tucked into their neckline, but we kids just wiped our hands on our shorts or rinsed off with the garden hose. Eating without table manners and running around the yard barefoot with the cousins was the very best of times.

# PICNIC MENUS

FRIED CHICKEN
POTATOES IN MUSTARD VINAIGRETTE WITH FRESH HERBS
SLICED WATERMELON

TOMATO, BASIL, AND MOZZARELLA WITH VINAIGRETTE ON ROLLS
BROWNIES

ROAST BEEF, LETTUCE, AND MAYONNAISE WITH HORSERADISH ON A BAGUETTE
CHOCOLATE-CHIP COOKIES

TUNA SALAD, RED ONION, AND SPROUTS ON WHOLE-GRAIN BREAD
NECTARINES AND PLUMS

TURKEY, AVOCADO, TOMATOES, AND CUCUMBERS IN A TORTILLA WRAP
GUACAMOLE AND CHIPS

FUSILLI WITH BASIL PESTO

CHERRY TOMATOES

HONEYDEW

COUSCOUS WITH ROASTED ASPARAGUS, TOMATOES, AND RED ONION

ROAST CHICKEN

BLONDIES

PEANUT BUTTER AND SLICED APPLE SANDWICHES

GRAPES

BREAD OR CRACKERS AND ASSORTED CHEESE

OLIVES

APRICOTS OR FIGS

**WHERE I** grew up in North Carolina, barbecue was eaten as a sandwich. Essentially it was pork cooked till it was falling-apart-soft and then chopped real fine and put on a bun—a white Sunbeam hamburger bun. On top of the pork, we'd pour some sauce and pile on coleslaw. You couldn't eat the thing without making a terrible mess. The very definition of finger-lickin' good, barbecue was divine.

My preferential topping was a sauce available only at the Boar and Castle, a drive-in with curbside service. For teenagers, the Boar and Castle was a rite-of-passage sort of place. The second that Ginny Ray Legare, the first in our girlfriend clique to turn sixteen, passed her driver's test, we piled in her daddy's car and drove to the Boar and Castle, where she pulled into the lighted section of the parking lot—as far as possible from an unlit area where reputations were lost or at least gossiped about on Monday at school. Anyhow, the carhops would come around, hang a tray on the driver's car window, and take our order. Whatever we ordered—Castleburger, buttered steak sandwich, onion rings—came smothered in Boar and Castle sauce. That sauce had a tart-sweet taste all its own, the result of some mysterious combination of spices and tomatoes.

The Boar and Castle closed decades ago, but an enterprising soul secured the recipe and distributed the sauce in Tabasco-size bottles, which I bought up by the dozen every time I'd

A LARGE BAGUETTE or hero can be the foundation of a picnic for children as well as adults. Fill half the roll with plain roast beef for the kids; add Cheddar, grainy mustard, lettuce, and tomatoes to the other half for adults.

visit family back in Greensboro. I used to travel with Bubble Wrap just so I could bring them home without breakage. Now I've learned B&C sauce is no more. But thanks to the Carolina Sauce company, I'm tasting substitutes, including Thomas's, which is packaged quite similarly to B&C. Hmmm.

The best way to serve barbecue, by the way—and I've learned this the hard way—is to set out an oilcloth that can be wiped down with a sponge when everybody's done. True oilcloth, which was heavy cotton duck or canvas treated with linseed oil, is hard to come by these days; flannel-backed vinyl, cut to size, is what passes for oilcloth, and in terms of indestructibility, you can't go wrong. My own "oilcloth" is a cotton weave that's been PVC-coated for water-resistance and durability. I found it in Santa Barbara, California, in a fabric place that advertised mill ends, and I bought the whole bolt of it—about twelve feet. It covers my dining table like a giant place mat, which is what I want to do when barbecue is on the menu.

from the linen closet

*Robin Wright*

In the days of my youth, my parents would load my sister, brothers, and me into our Rambler station wagon and off we'd go to spend the weekend at Aunt Skeeter and Uncle Toby's. During the three-hour drive that seemed to take all day, we entertained ourselves by playing the license-plate game. (When Alaska became a state in '59, we all wanted to be the first to spy that one. But in all the years we took that trip, we never saw a car from Alaska.)

We loved visiting our aunt and uncle because we got to feed the pigs and chickens, pick gooseberries, pet litters of kittens, and play games on huge concrete blocks that were colored shades of pink, red, and green. Marigold and portulaca grew between each slab, so it was a real challenge (but loads of fun!) to bounce our little red balls, play jacks, jump rope, and hopscotch, all the while trying to avoid stepping on the flowers.

In the heat of the afternoon, we'd be summoned inside to cool off. A gracious hostess, Aunt Skeeter would offer us a platter of homemade cookies, slices of cake, and fresh lemonade served in aluminum tumblers, each wearing a jacket she'd crocheted.

Aunt Skeeter was very talented with a needle. She sewed all her own clothes, including the aprons she wore over her day dresses, made beautiful quilts, embroidered pieces, and crocheted tablecloths. I remember her dipping the crochet pieces in a starch solution made out of flour and water and placing the pieces outside in the sun. Every once in a while, we'd go outside and fluff up the peaks of the ruffles until they dried stiff as a board.

I have many pieces of her needlework—some are probably one hundred years old now—including a set of sheets with crochet trim that she embroidered as a wedding gift for my husband and me. I keep these cherished items in a cedar chest that was once hers. I always felt a special bond with Aunt Skeeter, and each time I open the lid to retrieve a cloth or quilt, that bond is renewed. I'm sure that it is from her that I inherited my love for sewing and creating with fabric.

**WHILE I** was attending the "University of Southern Hospitality," I came to understand an altogether different kind of picnic, one involving starched white linen, the family silver, and hired help to serve it all. I'd met a guy who invited me to the steeplechase races in Aiken, South Carolina. This was a very la-di-da event, I learned from some other girls, and so I dressed my very best, in heels and hose, with a pair of white gloves in my purse just in case. My date arrived looking movie-star handsome, in a white shirt and navy blazer with a crisply ironed handkerchief tucked in his pocket just so, and Weejuns sans socks. At the steeplechase, we sat on wooden bleachers and watched a race or two, and then we went back to his car, where a proper tailgate awaited us. The help had brought a table and set it up on the grassy lawn with linen, china, silver, and crystal. I don't remember what we ate but I distinctly remember the odd sensation of being waited on out there with the horses around us. It was a different tradition than I was used to, that's for sure.

### FIRE UP THE GRILL!

Certain cloths of mine get assigned to outdoor duty simply because they're big enough to cover a picnic table—and can handle all manner of abuse.

This blue-and-teal plaid is one of them. I'm guessing it's from the '60s, not only because of the color and design but because it's a stiff cotton/synthetic blend. I don't particularly like the feel of it, but it does wear like iron.

And it gives me an excuse to wear my Hot Mitt Pocket Apron. I just love what that pocket does for the organza, tying together the plaid sash and border. The orangey-yellow piping adds such warmth, too. I use cloth napkins in this same hue to warm up the tablecloth, though it's the very coolness of that blue that makes the picnic so inviting on a hot summer night.

# How to Pack a Picnic

Whether you're packing a bag of sandwiches and a jug of lemonade or an herb-roasted chicken and a magnum of champagne, a picnic succeeds based on how well you've kitted it out. Can you carry it easily? Set it up in style? Serve it with grace? Clean it up without burdening the local dumpster and our planet? Here are some strategic pointers:

*In a hamper, basket, backpack, canvas tote, or combination of carriers:*

Ground cover (oilcloth or plastic)

Blanket, quilt, or tablecloth

Napkins—paper if you must, preferably cloth

Glasses or cups—unbreakable, but not Styrofoam or disposable plastic

Plates—melamine or other nondisposable picnicware

Corkscrew or bottle opener

Metal utensils (including serving spoons and a kitchen knife) wrapped in dish towels or napkins

Salt, pepper, condiments

Trash bag

Aluminum foil

Matches

First aid (antibiotic ointment, Band-Aids, insect repellant, sunscreen, cortisone cream, tweezers, Ace bandage)

Swiss Army knife

*In a thermal plastic jug (prechilled):*

Cold nonalcoholic beverage

STITCH FOUR TO six bandanas into a square and use it to line your picnic basket. With the food removed, the liner becomes a picnic cloth.

*In a sturdy cooler that can double as a seat or table, or in thermal totes:*

Perishables—ready-to-cook in resealable plastic bags

Prepared foods—ready-to-serve in plastic containers

Freezer packs under and over perishables

Wine bottles

Enough airspace to keep everything chilled—don't overpack!

*Optional:*

Folding tables and chairs

As an adult, of course, I learned that tailgating for most people meant gathering for a sporting event in a parking lot with tons of friends and acquaintances, either to support a team or a good cause. I'm still astonished at the amount of planning that goes into these affairs; they are not thrown together by any means. The ones I've been to begin with breakfast, because of course you've got to get there super-early to secure a good spot for the whole gang. The Bloody Marys and coffee and rolls have been prepared ahead of time, but the lunch that follows is invariably cooked right on the spot and served in courses. Tables and chairs will come out of someone's truck and be completely decorated with cloth, silverware, even candelabra. I've seen people set up these Ali Baba–like tents, complete with furniture and chandeliers. Otherwise you've got lounging furniture, or hammocks set up on stands, so that everyone can settle in for a day of nibbling, drinking, and milling around. Going into the stadium for the actual event is optional: Someone's got a television hooked up so you can watch the game right there in the parking lot, or listen to it on the stereo, and keep right on nibbling and drinking and cheering wildly whenever the home team scores. What makes it all possible is the generator running full tilt in the host vehicle, positioned up front so that it doesn't disturb the guests. The only thing the host or the core group of organizers does not bring is a facility. Faced with "holding it" for the entire day or compromising my plumbing standards and using the porta-potties in the parking lot, I find it helpful to go to such parties with my own little roll of tp (available at camping stores) and the right mind-set— as if I'm at a KOA Kampground.

A CLOTH NAPKIN makes a picnic of even the simplest bagged lunch.

**THESE DAYS** I'm much more inclined to attend—or host—the genteel outdoor affair, which more resembles a garden party than picnicking. I love to throw a garden party, perhaps because I've got a bevy of bright, colorful floral cloths. The best thing about these cloths, aside from their fantastic palette of colors, is the size of so many of them: They're 46 to 48 inches square, big enough to cover a card table. To me, that smallish size is a plus, because it allows me to do what I do best: mix and match, layer and design.

What inspires me about the striped cloth with the floral border, for instance, is the way the design moves from a dense lattice to another variation on the stripes to a single eight-inch square of flowers at the very center. It just begs to be made the centerpiece of my ensemble. I've built tables around the unusual salmon pink cloth (see page 84), too, probably because the daffodil motif is not what you'd expect with these colors. The hues of this green-and-white one with the peony motif I love so much that I painted my kitchen in those colors. It's rare that I'll use a cloth by itself, although I think the strong graphics of the pineapple cloth (see page 90) make it a stand-alone. Maybe white napkins, just to anchor it.

I featured the entire collection during our twenty-fifth wedding anniversary party, which we held outside in late fall. Hank and I rented around ten tables that sat six, and ten white rental cloths. I layered my favorite cloths on top, accented them with napkins, and set them with silver and glassware the night before. Gazing out upon them from an upstairs window, I was so excited by the effect, I could hardly sleep!

One of the most genteel affairs that Hank and I regularly attend is the President's Tailgate that our friends Kathryn and Bruce Grube throw every year in Statesboro, Georgia. Bruce is the president of Georgia Southern University, and he and Kathryn organize elegant tailgates throughout the school's football season. Held in the enclosed president's box that overlooks the open stadium, these affairs are beautifully done. White linen, silver chafing dishes, platters, and the perfect low-gracing flower arrangement adorn

## VINTAGE PICNIC ENSEMBLE

On my way home from the grocery the other day, I passed an Estate Sale sign in the front yard of a sweet bungalow-type house. The era of the neighborhood signaled that the goods for sale would likely include household linens. Sure enough, I came across this pretty blue and white check—"vintage" '60s, yet the organdy was a '50s trend. The apron has a small tear where the left tie is sewn to the apron's waistband—a common condition when the least substantial fabric was used to sew the part of the apron that is constantly pulled—but a cinch to fix. The cloth is a fifty-inch square. I'd love to set this up outside and top it with a white ceramic vase filled with daisies. Because the check is somewhat see-through, I'd set another cloth down first and layer this one on top. I bought the whole ensemble, including matching napkins, for such a pittance, I felt bad. Using it with joy will balance things out.

the buffet table. China and cloth napkins are refreshed without the slightest interruption. Although the menu changes, sacrosanct is the Trinity—deviled eggs, pimiento cheese on triangles of crustless white bread, and fried chicken—and guests must (!) eat one of each, because doing so brings the team good luck. One time, with the score tied, Kathryn noted who had or hadn't eaten their Trinity, and Hank, not a fan of pimiento cheese but nonetheless a team player, admitted he'd been remiss. Just as he swallowed his triangle, Georgia Southern scored the winning touchdown.

The focus here isn't on drinking, which I appreciate. You can fix yourself a plate, sit down to watch the game, or go outside and socialize. Moseying around, nibbling, and conversing—my three favorite things—are still what define a tailgate or picnic for me, no matter where it's held and no matter what's served.

**FOURTH OF JULY** picnics, I have always thought, needn't be limited to the holiday. That's because I have a penchant for the color scheme, red, white, and blue, and cannot see why so many of my favorite cloths should get only one day a year to make an appearance. My fixation probably started when I was a child and I'd accompany my mother to the Piggly Wiggly, which was our grocery store. Each year around the Fourth, the store would mount this tremendous display in the frozen food section, with red, white, and blue crepe paper twined all over the place and bunting and boxes of sparklers.

The Blue Tulip cloth is the perfect color combination, and it's in perfect condition. It was part of my mother-in-law's collection, although I never saw her use it. It's a heavy, tight weave, like damask, but white damask is what she used on her dining room table and this is far too huge for her to have put it on her dinette table. I'm inclined to use it on top of the little bridge cloth with a cherry design because it was folded in a drawer so long it's got yellowing. I'd layer them so you'd just see the corners of the bridge cloth hanging down.

Which is another thing about my collection: If I like a pattern or a color, I pay no mind to imperfections like yellowing or tears or fraying hems. I'm like those women of the '30s and '40s: I throw nothing away, and I pick up what others have thrown out. That piece of red-and-white feed sack? I may use it to create little napkin pockets for a bridge cloth, one on each corner. And that red-and-white picnic weave (see page 81)? I'm going to make a silverware pocket out of it, something to put my flatware in and roll up for a picnic as part of the display.

from the linen closet

## Melinda Marshall

*I* don't have a picnic table. I certainly don't have one that seats eight. But this didn't stop my mother from bequeathing the Family Picnic Cloth, a black-and-white gingham, to me on one of her rare visits. So now when she spends a night or two with us, I make sure to unfurl the thing on my formal dining room table, which it happens to cover rather nicely. All that's missing are the people who used to sit around it: my five brothers, assorted cousins visiting from California, friends of ours from school, bachelor teachers my mother had taken under wing, my grandparents, who lived next door, and my long-suffering father.

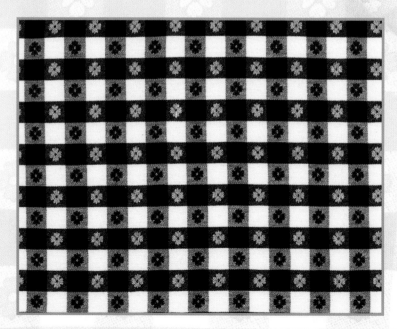

The most amazing thing about this cloth is that it bears no stains. I don't know how this is possible, given the gallons of barbecue sauce that passed over it. The sauce was homemade, from a recipe my mother found in a *Better Homes & Gardens* mailer of free recipes, and just the tangy smell of it bubbling on the stove tipped us off to the fact we'd be eating dinner "out at the picnic table" under the pin oak. It also alerted Jay, my youngest brother, that he was on grilling duty. Jay loved to eat and, in a stroke of genius, my parents had given him a Happy Cooker one year for his birthday. I can see him still, a hulking teenager, crouched over this little charcoal brazier with his water gun, spritzing the coals lest they blacken the chicken he was tending.

Although the cloth has moved indoors, it tends to dictate picnic-y menus. I grill chicken, I make the Famous Family Sauce, and, as my mother did, I set out candles and we talk around the table until they burn into puddles. Thankfully, there are no mosquitoes to drive us away.

One day, perhaps, a child of mine will get the picnic cloth and restore it to its rightful place under a pin oak somewhere. But I can't promise there won't be stains.

# part four

# THERE'S NO PLACE LIKE HOME

*"Thanksgiving dinner was good. Pa had shot a
wild goose for it. Ma had to stew the goose because
there was no fireplace, and no oven in the little
stove. But she made dumplings in the gravy. There
were corn dodgers and mashed potatoes. There
were butter and milk and stewed dried plums."*

—Laura Ingalls Wilder, *On the Banks of Plum Creek*

**SINCE COLONIAL** times in this country, a cloth on the table has always signified a
better-than-usual dinner—or at least better-than-usual company. A cloth meant it was someone's birthday, or an anniversary; it was Thanksgiving or Christmas; it was Sunday dinner
or Friday Shabbat. The "company cloth" for most families was white or off-white and made
of linen, silk, cotton, or a combination of these
fibers. For well-to-do families, only
damask—dense linen or silk cloth
with intricate patterns or scenes
reverse-woven into it—would do.

Damask was the tablecloth
everyone aspired to own. Expensive to produce, and difficult to
launder and iron, damask linen gave
wealthy families here as well as in

## KNOW YOUR WEAVES

In weaving, the WEFT or woof is the yarn or thread drawn under and over the parallel WARP threads on a loom to make fabric. The oldest weaving technique, PLAIN WEAVE, is one in which the weft yarns simply alternate over and under the warp yarns. Plain weave is used in lots of different fabric types, including cambric, percale, seersucker, and tweed. In TWILL WEAVE, the most commonly used weave after plain weave, the weft yarns go over one and under two or more warp yarns, creating a diagonal pattern. Herringbone, houndstooth, gabardine, serge, chino, and denim are all types of twill weaves.

CAMBRIC is a closely woven, soft cotton or linen fabric used in lighter weights for aprons; its slightly glossy finish on one side is produced by *calendering*, or passing the cloth between a series of heated rollers. CALICO originally referred to printed cloths originating in Calcutta, India, but now the term usually means an unbleached, inexpensive textile made of cotton or a cotton/synthetic

Europe new ways to impress their guests. The best-quality damask was linen and came from Ireland, which at one point was the flax-growing center of Europe, and had a luster and weight unlike anything else on the market. "Double damask" commanded the highest prices because the weave packed in twice as many threads, and the higher thread count enabled very intricate designs. As Jacquard looms became

blend. CHINTZ, a glazed, plain-weave cotton, is multiply printed in bright colors, usually in a floral design.

Made of silk, rayon, linen, cotton, or a combination of fibers, DAMASK fabric gets its name from Damascus, the city famous for its beautiful textiles as early as the twelfth century. Damask was known originally as *figured* or *storied damask* because it reproduced a painting or depicted a narrative. Early themes were mostly religious and the cloths were often used for altars; coats-of-arms and family crests were popular damask designs, a tradition that survives today in the signature monogrammed napkins and linens of fine hotels. Damask is usually white or one or two colors only. Unlike BROCADE, which is a colorful, heavy fabric with raised embroidery and very often ornamental gold or silver threads, or TAPESTRY, a wool, cotton, or silk weave in which the parallel threads of the fabric are hidden completely by the weft, damask is reversible and lies flat. The JACQUARD LOOM, invented by Joseph Marie Jacquard in 1801, made it easier to change the patterns on a loom, and JACQUARD WEAVE is still the term applied to intricate designs made in brocade, damask, and tapestry.

more automated, and rayon took the place of silk, more Americans could afford damask; every self-respecting homemaker had at least one oceanic cloth to put on the dining room table when her husband's boss came to dinner. If it wasn't of the highest quality, well—it still *looked* classy.

Up until the '60s, in fact, the tradition of inheriting, giving, or receiving damask linen as a wedding present persisted. It was the fabric of every important occasion, holiday, and rite of passage. For my senior prom in 1966, in fact, my parents prepared and served a formal dinner—on the family damask, of course—for me and my best friends Ginny Ray Legare, Lollie Lake, Huttie Kent, Lynnie Frierson, and Judy Elstrom, and our dates. In our formal wear, seated at a formal dining table, we felt so grown up. No one's parents had ever done such a thing. And when we get together, we still talk about it.

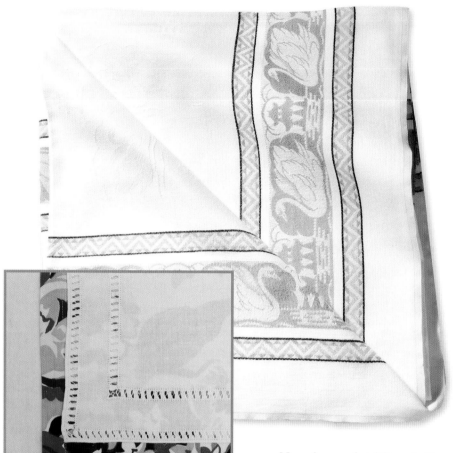

Nowadays, we feel differently. You can pick up damask linens for a song. Even the coveted Irish weaves are all over the secondhand market and eBay, for the simple reason that no one wants to have to store and take care of something that is rarely, if ever, used. The very factors that made damask linens once so valuable are what today render them obsolete: They're large, heavy, and ornate. Despite the beauty of their woven design, they're white or off-white—rather *boring*, frankly. They're perceived as old-fashioned, the sort of table dressing that made dinner parties uptight and family gatherings overly formal. And laundering them, let alone ironing them, is either a chore or an expense most of us don't want to undertake.

I buy them up. I've gotten rid of other things, files and papers and such, to make room for them. Why? Because to touch such linens is to love them. Few weaves hold up to countless launderings the way damask does. The linens I've got are so lusciously soft that, even if they're stained, I foresee getting lots of use out of them as hand toweling or napkins. I'm not crazy about white, but some of the patterns woven into them are truly amazing, and the way the cloth drapes on a table just can't be beat. I'll use damask as my foundation, using its vastness to cover unsightly table legs or makeshift furniture. Once the damask is down, I have a nice blank canvas to "paint" with an array of more captivating cloths: striped towels, handworked hankies, scenic panels from vintage curtains, bold place mats, colorful runners, embroidered napkins, and crocheted doilies. In fact, I've come to see a huge white expanse of damask as the equivalent of the little black dress: You can do marvelous things with it, for all manner of occasions. Depending on how you accessorize it, you can dress it up or down. And dressed up, it never looks dated or fusty.

I like to use my smaller pieces in concert with one another to create different looks, or different moods. For instance, the same fine white linen place mat can adorn my damask either by itself, or on top of a floral runner. Either way, you see its lovely handwork, but one is more formal and the other, more festive. I made the floral runner (opposite page) from a curtain someone really cherished; if you look closely you can see where a rip was expertly repaired. Since I've got lots of that curtain fabric, I might crisscross the table with runners for a startling plaid effect, all anchored with the white place mats that echo the white damask. Similarly, I've created bold runners by taking large square napkins and positioning them as a series of diamond shapes on top of the damask.

*The earliest settlers in America took their meals at a* bord *or* borde*—literally a wooden plank or two, set on a trestle. This arrangement made sense because it could be dismantled after dining to make room for other activities—an important consideration in modest dwellings. To "set the table" for dinner meant, literally, to set trestle and board in front of those who intended to dine. We also reference that early arrangement whenever we speak of "room and board."*

# *Napkins*
## THROUGH HISTORY

The Romans are credited with inventing napkins, which proved essential tools to civilized dining until forks came into use in the early seventeenth century. People ate with their fingers, and since much eating was done while reclining, a napkin helped minimize the inevitable mess. There were two kinds of napkins, in fact: A hankie-size one for mopping the sweat from your brow, and a large one to protect your clothing as food moved from hand to mouth. The large one was then used as a wrap for guests to take home leftovers—the first doggie bag. It wasn't uncommon for diners at a table to share a napkin. Or, for that matter, to wipe their fingers and mouths on the tablecloth.

The fashion of large napkins persisted through the Middle Ages, at least in homes where the family could afford to cover the table (and wish the cloth to be spared). In a fifteenth-century depiction of *The Last Supper*, several diners are sharing a length of linen as long as the table—what we would call a "runner" today, but clearly a napkin under the circumstances. Later paintings from the Renaissance show exuberant diners sporting vast white napkins tied about their waists or worn almost like an apron. Knives and spoons and fingers were the utensils of the day.

The fork, though introduced in the early seventeenth century, didn't catch on until the eighteenth. But once everyone had gotten the hang of it (the Italians were the first to embrace the fork), napkins began to shrink in size and grow in ornamentation. The French, in particular, seized on the napkin as the vehicle for ostentation, adding breathtaking embroidery, cutwork, and lace adornment. By the eighteenth century, in Europe at least, the napkin was more of a social nicety than necessity, a means of dressing up the table, not wiping down the guests. The smaller and fancier the napkin, the more imperative it was that one ate in such a manner as to not require its use.

Today, fortunately, the trend toward ever-tinier napkins has reversed a bit. We still want a square of cloth between us and our meal, not because we eat with our fingers but because we'd rather protect our dry-clean-only blouse from the tomato bisque. The smallest napkins— the cocktail, or beverage, napkin—are under 5 inches square. Luncheon napkins range in size from 6 to 12 inches. What was once considered a luncheon napkin—18 inches square—is more the norm for dinner, although technically 22 inches is the minimum size for formal gatherings. Hardly the 40-inch "lapkin" of our forebears, but it will have to do!

Ladies Handkerchiefs

Harriet

Hankies

**OR I'LL** go in the other direction, and use the expanse of white cloth to feature my collection of handkerchiefs. They're way too pretty to keep in a box or drawer, and I've got tons of them. As a girl, I always had a hankie in my purse. I can remember receiving boxes of them as gifts, embroidered with, say, days of the week motifs, and I remember how delighted I was by their beauty. My European grandmother wouldn't have dreamed of going out of the house without a perfumed handkerchief tucked in her corset or purse: It was the mark of a lady. I've since come to understand that handkerchiefs, like napkins, were not simply utilitarian. They were critical opportunities for a woman to express herself through her choice of color and fabric and her needle art. That's why I collect them: The women who embroidered their monograms or scalloped these edges may have lived fifty, sixty, or

## from the linen closet

### Ellen Baker

My father was the youngest person ever made a vice president of J. Walter Thompson, the advertising agency. He was sent out, as a bachelor, to open their San Francisco office in 1932, and, during those halcyon prewar days, hobnobbed with the Bay Area's social elite. It was his job to entertain clients, and, rumor has it, one of them was William Randolph Hearst. Eventually he met my mother, and they opened their own advertising agency in New York, where they had very successful careers.

After his death in 1968, my mother moved to a one-bedroom apartment. As I was establishing my first home and beginning to do serious entertaining (more than a bottle of wine with cheese and crackers), she began giving me gifts of silver, Wedgwood china, and table linens. Among the linens were some place mats I had never seen before: lovely pale green linen with a tailored white border and *RLB*, my father's initials, done in a classic art deco font. When I asked her why they were only my father's initials, she explained that they had belonged to him when he was hosting lavish dinner parties in San Francisco. Those place mats, no doubt from Gump's, the grand old San Fran department store, brought to mind my father as I imagined him in those days, six foot three, blue-eyed, and dark-haired—like a movie star. He had always loved the finer things in life that his success brought him. Of course he had his own monogrammed linen! And not a stain on them—he was very fastidious.

I took them home, washed them in Woolite, carefully ironed them, and began using them as he did for lavish gatherings. Time for ironing linens and polishing silver seems as elusive as time for elaborate dinner parties now, but I've kept those place mats looking as crisp and fresh as they did in the '30s—so that I can take them to *Antiques Roadshow* some day.

seventy years ago, but they come alive for me when I admire and share their work. I find the miniscule detailing on tiny white hankies especially enchanting. One of these hankies makes the perfect gift for a teenaged girl when wrapped around a ten-dollar bill and tied with a ribbon and sprig of lavender . . . because a lady is never without a hanky and cab fare home. Colored ones I keep for my dinner table, because the damask makes such a great easel for displaying their art. My art deco hankie has quite the impact, I think, when framed by the elaborate edging of a huckaback towel folded underneath it. And that goldenrod decoration? It's crochet, plus rickrack, then more crochet, then more rickrack, and one last row of crochet.

## SUNDAY DINNER

Sunday dinner, where I grew up, was the meal taken after church. Being Jewish, we didn't go to church, although we attended Sunday school. Retrieved at noon by my father or Mr. Goss, who also had a huge station wagon (but only three children), and with whom my parents traded off pick-up duty, we'd return home to the everyday fare of sandwiches, chips, and milk. But I was well acquainted with the tradition of Sunday dinner, having girlfriends who invited me into their midst. I remember what a family affair it was, with everybody taking orders from their apron-clad mother and helping to get the meal on the table. And what a meal: roast chicken or pot roast, greens, sweet potato casserole or mashed potatoes and gravy, and rolls, biscuits, or corn bread and dessert. The family would tuck in as though it were the last meal of the day, because it was. (Supper would be Campbell's soup and a butter sandwich.) I recall the relaxed atmosphere, the adults talking and smoking at the table, the younger kids running around in the yard after changing out of their Sunday best, and my friend and I retiring to her bedroom to read movie-star magazines and practice the latest dance steps we'd seen on American Bandstand.

If I were hosting Sunday dinner, I'd wear an apron like this one with the matching hot pads—perfect for bringing a still-bubbling baked pie to the table. Or this one with the sunbonnet pocket. I'm not sure how vintage it is—the '50s, I'm guessing—because that embroidered flower crops up on a lot of my linens, from all eras. But the cheery yellow trim puts me in mind of midday feasts and the families that assembled around them.

**SOME OF** my damask do-overs have been inspired by collectibles that intrigued me. A palm-size red plastic man's hat, for instance, was part of a grab bag I bought from Terry Stuive, an antique dealer here in Pueblo. He explained that when you wanted to give someone a new Stetson (generic for "hat" out West), the store provided this little stand-in, because the hat itself had to be custom-fitted to the recipient. A charming custom, I thought— one that promptly inspired me to get out this fabric featuring different cowboy scenes. Someone had cut up curtains into these pictorial squares, perhaps for pillows or a quilt, and then never got around to finishing the project. I ironed under their unfinished edges and placed them atop dish towels whose red stripes provided a nice framework for the scene. To complete the ensemble, I chose a damask napkin to complement the foundation cloth and add a bit of contrasting formality. The whole arrangement is reminiscent of how we used to reward our boys, when they were young, for having completed a task above and beyond what was required of them. Money was never involved. Instead, to honor their accomplishment and show them we'd noticed their extra effort, they'd be granted some privilege—a friend over for dinner and then bowling or a movie

without us in attendance. And I'd make their place at the dinner table extra special. I think this cowboy ensemble would have done just that!

Not all of my do-overs involve damask, either. Some of my cotton cloths are so formal, I just feel the need to lighten their impact. My Asian dinner cloth seemed rather chilly to me, with its bold geometric border and cool blue background. The pattern itself—the demure woman under the parasol pretending not to notice her admirer, above—reminded me of *The King and I*, which, along with fortune cookies at a Chinese restaurant, was the extent of my knowledge of the Far East back in the '50s. But as soon as I put that apple green fabric under it, wow! The whole mood of it lifted.

## from the linen closet

### Erin Owens

In April 2001, we celebrated my parents' fiftieth wedding anniversary in New Orleans, where they were married, and where my family had lived for generations. It seemed only fitting that I, who had inherited my mother's trousseau of fine linens, should plan a party featuring them—the damask, jacquard, embroidered, cutout linen, and printed cotton sets that would easily cover a series of large formal tables. My mother had taken great care of these cloth treasures; in turn, I had stored the napkins in the drawers of my Duncan Phyfe sideboard, which I inherited from my grandmother, and hung the cloths in a special airy room designated as the official "linen closet."

I had the most fun putting together the tables for the party I had planned. Not since my parents' wedding, I believe, had all the family linen, china, and crystal appeared in such a magnificent display. Noritake, Lenox, Waterford, and Royal Doulton graced the damask-covered tables that I set for the forty-eight guests. On each table, I arranged roses in Mc-Coy pottery vases.

And the event itself was truly memorable: Fine food, heartfelt toasts from good friends, children, and grandchildren, and poems written for the occasion transported us on a sentimental journey back to the New Orleans of old. Following cocktails served in our gazebo, we dined on cream of fresh tomato soup, spring greens with strips of beef tenderloin, walnuts and blue cheese with vinaigrette dressing, duchess potatoes, dilled green beans, poached salmon, and the most delicious lemon curd–filled cake with buttercream icing.

I am so glad we mounted this effort, because so much of what was— our family, and our city—is now gone forever. My beloved mother, wheelchair-bound then and struggling with the debilitating effects of disease, passed away seven months after the anniversary dinner. Four years later, New Orleans as I knew it was swept away by the levee-breaching waters of Katrina. Today, as I continue to grieve, I turn to the linens that have passed from one generation to the next and feel the joy and the strength that come from being part of this powerful legacy.

**I'M ALWAYS** one for changing the dinner mood. Sometimes you've had words with your partner, or it's just been that kind of day, when everybody would benefit from the conversation taking a different direction. What if you put out books? Just their title or cover would spark discussion. I have a collection of early readers—Dick and Jane, Tip and Muff—that's unbelievable. I've put out record albums, too. And marbles. Anything that'll bring a smile. Maybe it's a holdover from my youth, when my parents insisted the baby of the house be allowed to assail us with jokes from her birthday present, *101 Elephant Jokes.* As the youngest of six, Carol, then nine, could never stump us with a Knock-Knock or Little Moron joke, because we'd heard them all. But elephant jokes were brand new. So 101 dinners began with her reading out of her book. How does an elephant hide in a strawberry patch? He wears red shoes.

I'd be tempted to put a book of jokes on my art deco dinner cloth, just to lighten its somber mood. I do love its deep cranberry hue, and I know, given its heavy weave, its impeccable condition, and its age, that it's a valuable cloth. But the griffins-and-lyre motif is a bit dark, even scary-looking. The apple-green cloth underneath would help brighten and lighten it. Or just some unexpected object like this green-jacketed book from 1948, which promises to share "perfected methods of spouse-torture." Yay, my kind of fun!

**WHILE MY** dinner cloths and napkins may look valuable, quite a few are what I'd call "great pretenders." I don't buy things for what they may be worth to someone else; I let my heart and my eye tell me what to collect. A perfect example: my rose-colored damask. The cotton one with the silvery design is from the '30s, and it was available in yellow, green, and ecru as well as deep rose. I thought it was made of silk when I bought it, because of its lovely feel and drape, but I've since learned that the woven pattern is rayon—one of the first-ever man-made fibers. Far from being disappointed, I felt I'd been granted the right to use it without anxiety. The pink-and-white dinner cloth from the 1920s—what I call my carnation cloth— similarly looks a lot nicer than it really is. It's damask: The carnation motif is woven into it,

thanks to the innovations made possible by Jacquard looms. But it's an uneven, utilitarian weave, meant to be affordable. The hand hemming on each end tells me it was sold as yardage. I love to use it on all manner of occasions because, along with my damask napkins, it makes such a pretty table. I can't resist adding crocheted teacups as place-card holders.

In the same spirit, I'd use my American Beauty cloth. It may have had real value once, but I suspect it's been bleached, because there's a phantom pattern on it, behind the three rows of red roses. American Beauty was a Wilendur cloth made in the '40s as both yardage and finished goods. Mine is finished by machine, so I think it was part of a boxed set originally. I like pairing it with these white napkins because they have the same weave. And the leafy green detail on my set of little plastic salt-and-peppers is the perfect complement.

**IF CANDLES PUDDLE** *on your tablecloth, don't touch the wax until it's hardened, because smearing it in makes it worse. Take the whole cloth and stick it in the freezer. That makes the wax brittle enough to chip off. Remove remaining wax by applying a warm iron to the area over paper towels. If using colored candles, set the holder on a tray or plate to catch any drips; otherwise, the dye may leave a permanent stain.*

**SOME OF** my dinner cloths, I've learned, weren't necessarily even made for the table. The white one with blue stripes and a scalloped edge, textile collector Mariella Warner tells me, may just as easily have served as a summertime coverlet for a bed. Nonetheless, because it's from the 1920s, it has a certain elegance I admire. I'd probably trot out my silver candelabra, the ones I inherited from Trudy and Bert, European cousins of Hank's, as a centerpiece, and fill the branches with different colored candles to dispel its otherwise stuffy demeanor.

## from the linen closet
### Judith McGinnis

Our clan dined communally three times a year: Easter, Christmas, and my grandmother's birthday. This was quite a feat, because my grandmother, Miss Fanny, had seven children and thirty some grandchildren. To seat us all together meant using every leaf on the grand oak table and a few card tables besides.

It also meant using every piece of family linen, ancient china, and heirloom crystal. We girl cousins were conscribed to prepare the table. Jobs were assigned by age. The youngest were sent to the linen press to fetch tablecloths and napkins; one would lift the press board while another pulled cool, flat damask from underneath. Slightly older cousins demonstrated with pride how to flick one hem of the cloth and send it cascading down the length of the table, floating into place. Next came the silver stewards, girls of ten or so who had taken at least one turn on polishing day with the housekeeper. Miss Fanny not only showed us how and where to position each knife, fork, and spoon, but recounted the history of pieces passed down by her mother and grandmother. Finally the crystal was placed, a task reserved for the oldest girls who knew a water glass from a wine stem and were careful enough not to break them. Only Willie Mae was trusted to move the stacks of Haviland plates to the end of the buffet. Miss Fanny finished the tables with roses from her garden. At every step, she taught lessons from a Victorian world that no longer existed: the proper care of cut-work linen, where a fish fork goes, whether or not to set finger bowls. Such lessons in decorum brought us closer to her.

Finally, the women emerged from the kitchen, bearing great platters and bowls piled high. These meals were the work of fine Christian women in fierce competition: The elder women made Southern classics while the younger generation tried more exotic fare from between the checkerboard covers of *Better Homes & Gardens Cookbook*. Fried chicken or veal birds, peach cobbler or stuffed angel food cake—lucky for us, every one was a winner. My father was always the only man who contributed to the meal, specifically at dessert time when the side table groaned with goodies. His lemon icebox pies joined six-layer chocolate cake, Lane cake, Jeff Davis pie, blackberry trifle, and banana pudding. Thank goodness it was the 1960s and no one knew how bad any of this was for us.

When everyone staggered from the table, the plates, cutlery, and glassware were carefully cleared, rinsed, washed, and dried for the next occasion. As the evening deepened, we collected on Miss Fanny's porch to hear the elders tell and retell the family stories. Dominoes clicked and the porch swing, with babies carefully bedded down on it, squeaked in a lulling rhythm. Eventually, only the sound of rockers creaking on the porch boards carried over the hydrangeas. Drifting off to sleep on our pallets in the parlor, we had no idea that one day we would give anything to set Miss Fanny's table again.

**PURE UNADORNED** damask can be perfectly beautiful on its own, of course. My mother used it for all of our family celebrations and holidays, Thanksgiving being her favorite. The chores of preparation—from extending the table with the extra leaves, to washing dozens of glasses, to setting the table with every piece of china she had ever come by, including the Golden Wheat pattern that came in the Duz detergent box (perhaps one of the first Free Gift with Purchase promotions?)—had her humming a happy tune. Her main focus was to issue invitations to those who might not have anyplace else to go or lived too far from their own families. That might be my cousin Donnie and his college friends, or single acquaintances of my parents, or the family down the street experiencing a difficult time. "Let's make room for one more," she'd say, "because that's the one who really needs to be here." As a result, there'd be twelve or more of us at the main table, and "the baby girls" at the children's table.

My mother would get up at 5:00 a.m. to start trussing up the bird, peeling the onions, boiling the sweet potatoes, and making her signature apple pies, which tended to have more raisins and cinnamon than apples. She wasn't much of a cook, my mother—Butterball, Kraft, and Crisco were her favorite brands—but she reveled in making this meal by herself while we watched the Macy's Thanksgiving

Day Parade on television. At 1:00 p.m., all of us dressed in our best, we would gather 'round as my father ceremonially took up knife and fork to carve the turkey. Before we ate, it was my mother who offered the blessing—and to this day, I tear up thinking how eloquent she was. It didn't matter how bad a year she may have had, health-wise—and she had many. Looking around the table and seeing all the shining faces, she gave thanks in a way that you could just hear her happiness.

This is not to suggest our gatherings were right out of Norman Rockwell. I remember sitting at the Thanksgiving table across from my brother Paul one year and lobbing a forkful of mashed potato and gravy across that ocean of damask. To this day, I do not know what possessed me to do such a thing. I was a college freshman, and full of myself, I'm sure. The potatoes and gravy did not hit Paul but landed, instead, on the tablecloth. My father was out of his chair in two seconds. He swooped me from my seat, swatted my eighteen-year-old behind, and sent me out of the dining room and upstairs to my room, me screaming and crying all the way there. I was utterly humiliated. I couldn't believe I had done anything so stupid. Oh, to suffer so; at the least, I should have hit my mark!

That cloth wound up going to my sister Susan. I know she uses it for Thanksgiving, and always features the turkey salt-and-pepper set that Mama had used at our family Thanksgivings. They're not at all valuable—the sticker, "Made in Japan," is still affixed to the bottom of each—but they hold a lot of precious memories.

## from the linen closet
### Mimi Haskel Weil

Long before I moved into a home of my own, I had linens.

My grandmother, born in Bucharest, Romania, had owned as a young woman a fine millinery shop for the royalty and aristocracy of the city. Appearance was always important to her, whether in her attire or on her table. Even when she ate alone, she always set the table with cloth and china. So, it was natural for her to always gift me with linens. Some were her creations, while others were carefully chosen: My favorite is a cross-stitch with bound edges of blue crochet. My mother also loved to cross-stitch table cloths, and bequeathed them to me. In addition to these, I received tablecloths as wedding presents, some for formal dinners and luncheons and others for our everyday use, although I didn't yet have a home or a dining room table. The cloths all came with matching napkins.

Eventually, along with the house and dining room table, I acquired the room to store my cache of linens, which I drape on hangers that have a tube of thick cardboard or padding so the cloth isn't in direct contact with the hanger. Each hanger is marked according to size. A "0" on the hanger is for the cloths that are used without leaves in the table. Other hangers are marked "1" or "2" accordingly. The round cloths are for tables that are extended with boards set on card tables. Some cloths are labeled "Holiday." Cloths that are folded and stacked on shelves are for the breakfast room or patio tables.

And so today, when I open my linen closet, it is like opening a photo album of my life. The white cloth with the cross-stitch Sabbath symbols reminds me of the Shabbat tradition that defined Fridays for me and my husband, Stan, and our children. And next to it, fittingly, is the cloth that we used for Christmas, because following Stan's death, I married into an entirely different tradition. My husband, Bob, liked to put on a formal Christmas Day dinner for his children and grandchildren with holiday napkins, matching plates, and engraved place cards at each setting.

I manage both of these occasions on my own, now. I intend to do so as long as I'm able, in honor of my own grandmother. It was she who taught me, with her gifts of linen, to always welcome my guests with a beautifully set table.

## TURKEY POT PIE

6 tablespoons (¾ stick) salted butter

1 cup chopped onion

½ cup chopped celery

6 tablespoons all-purpose flour

2 cups chicken broth

1 cup half-and-half

2 cups potatoes, boiled, peeled, and diced

2 cups frozen mixed vegetables

2 cups shredded or diced cooked turkey

1 tablespoon dried sage

1 tablespoon dried parsley

Salt and pepper

1 unbaked pie crust (the boxed, rolled crusts found in the dairy case work great. My pot pie has only a top crust)

*A STAIN OR two doesn't necessarily ruin a cloth. If napkins have stains, iron them to let your guests know that what they're using has been laundered. When a cloth gets so stained you can't use it without feeling embarrassed, move it to the rag pile and head for the secondhand store. Buying replacements is a whole lot more fun than trying to get out gravy, ketchup, or red wine!*

I inherited my mother-in-law's damask, which in its own way is quite appropriate. Her cloth bears no stains, but not for lack of my trying to give it some. The first Thanksgiving that Hank and I were married, we spent with his family. Naturally, my mother-in-law put out her beautiful white damask and set it with her best china, silver, and crystal. Wanting to be the helpful new daughter-in-law, I reached across the cloth for the bowl of bourbon sweet potatoes, as requested by Uncle Gus, and knocked over a glass

Preheat the oven to 400°F. Grease a 9-inch square baking pan.

Melt the butter in a skillet over medium heat; add the onions and celery and stir until softened (2 to 3 minutes). Stir in the flour; continue stirring for 3 to 4 minutes to make a roux (resist turning up the heat—instead of being hurried along, the mixture will burn). Slowly pour in the chicken stock, stirring to combine; bring this mixture to a boil, then lower the heat to medium-low and simmer until the sauce thickens, about 4 minutes. Stir in the half-and-half. Season with salt and pepper. Add the vegetables, turkey, and spices, and stir until good and mixed. Adjust the seasoning as necessary.

Pour the filling into the prepared pan. Place the crust on top of the filling, tucking the edges into the pan to form a thick edge. Cut several vents in the top of the crust.

Place the pan on a baking sheet and bake until the crust is golden brown, 25 to 30 minutes.

of red wine. Everybody at the table stopped breathing. To make matters even worse, in my panic, I grabbed up a damask napkin and started blotting at the spreading stain. Somehow Else managed to undo my calamity. In that moment, however, I knew I would spend the rest of my life undoing that first impression.

I don't use it for Thanksgiving, necessarily, or Hanukkah or Passover, for that matter. At this point in my role as mother and wife, I'm for mixing things up—and making *that* my tradition. Gone are the days when, like my mother, I got up at the crack of dawn to put the turkey in. We'll eat at six-thirty or seven, not midday, because I don't see the point of putting away all that food only to have to get it out again as people's "stomach clocks" go off at their regular suppertime. I don't make the green-bean casserole with the crunchy onions on top, or the sweet potato casserole covered in marshmallows, or three different kinds of pie. Years ago a light bulb went

on in my head: Why do all this and come to the table too exhausted to enjoy it? And why program my family to expect these things, year in and year out? What was important was that we were together. When my boys went off to college thousands of miles away, and were unable to join us for Thanksgiving, I realized I needed to let go of convention even more. Our holiday table held less family and more people who, like my sons, lived too far away to go home. I would cook turkey, of course, and pie. But I would take the opportunity to try out a new recipe that never held a mini marshmallow or crunchy onion on top. If truth be told, the whole reason to cook the turkey, as far as I'm concerned, is to generate enough leftovers for pot pie. So that's what I set out last year.

In fact, I no longer limit celebrating Thanksgiving to just the November date. Since my boys live hither and yon, I've decided it simply makes no sense to put so much value on

the one day, especially because it's fraught with the possibility of disappointment. Weather might keep them from arriving, or they'll have made plans of their own with friends. I refuse to put them on the spot. My feeling is, whenever they show up, it's Thanksgiving. I've got a turkey in the freezer at all times. It can be February and it's Thanksgiving.

Like my mother, I offer a blessing. I may never be as well-spoken, but I feel as she did: incredibly grateful to have a home in which to celebrate, food enough to share, and loved ones around the table . . . even if the cloth covers a card table and the settings are a mishmash because we're in the middle of construction. (Notice, though, the turkey salt-and-pepper set, which was on hand because I'd borrowed it from my sister to photograph for this book!)

In my blessing I talk about grandparents no longer with us, and how we miss them. I reference the first Thanksgiving, prepared by the Pilgrims as a meal of gratitude. And I never fail to mention the women whose initials are immaculately embroidered on our napkins. Using needle and thread, they committed to cloth their personalities, talent, and souls. Their initials remind us that they, too, once assembled around a table of family and friends to rejoice in what they had wrought.

Like vintage aprons, these old pieces of linen celebrate the tireless industry, familial devotion, and enduring spirit of mothers and grandmothers the world over.

## from the linen closet
### Robin Dellabough

When they married in the early 1950s, my parents lived in Greenwich Village, wore black berets, turtlenecks, and blue jeans, wrote poetry, and painted. They had grape-stomping parties that led to vinegar more often than wine, and listened both to cool and red-hot jazz. They embraced what used to be called the Bohemian life.

Then their first child was born. And although I slept in a dresser drawer rather than in some fancy bassinet those first few months, my mother decided she had to start my hope chest immediately. She bought a piece of off-white linen, 60 by 100 inches, large enough to cover the dining table she already envisioned for me, and chose thread in shades of rust and turquoise. Working in old-fashioned cross-stitch, she painstakingly embroidered a wide border. Or at least she tried to embroider a wide border. Five more children and two moves interrupted her plan.

I discovered the unfinished tablecloth in the back of a closet when I was ten years old and working on my own embroidery project, a monogrammed handkerchief for my grandfather. When she explained what it was, I thought, *How silly to make something for someone twenty-five years in advance.* Then I decided it was a shame—and she should *be* ashamed—that she hadn't been able to complete it. It became a running joke between us, as periodically I'd ask, "How's my tablecloth coming along?" She'd answer, "Oh, I'm going to get to it when your brothers leave home . . . after I go back to school . . . when we come back from Greece . . . when I have more time."

Nearly twenty years passed. The day before my own wedding, I walked into my backyard in Berkeley, California, where I was living what used to

be called the hippie life. There, at a shower filled with balloons and flowers and friends, my mother handed me a box and, before I even opened it, knowing what I would find inside, every stitch made with love, I was moved to tears.

It's been thirty more years, and my mother has passed. The tablecloth is stained now with countless Thanksgiving gravies and candle wax, but I still use it on the special occasions when my brothers and sisters and their families are gathered in my house. I quietly finger the embroidery during dinner, sending a silent thank-you to my mother, who somehow found a way to transcend time.

# Reinventing Kitchen Linens

$\mathcal{N}$ot long ago, as a thank-you gift for a friend, I packaged up a vintage set of green Bakelite dominoes in a Chinese take-out container. What made the container as special as the gift was the circle of tablecloth I cut for it, gathering up the edges around the dominoes like a hobo bag. "I enjoyed the packaging as much as the surprise inside," my friend wrote back.

I never throw out "ruined" table linens for this very reason. Applying just a little ingenuity, and a few notions, I can give second lives to tablecloths, napkins, place mats, or dishtowels with too many stains or tears to put out for company. I'm handy with a sewing machine, but you don't have to be. Some of my favorite reinventions rely on these basic supplies:

Pinking shears

Therm O Web Iron-on Vinyl—a fusible, washable laminate

Wonder Under—a fusible adhesive you iron onto fabric

Assorted ribbons

Assorted buttons

Assorted rickrack

Card stock, or heavyweight paper for note cards

Ruler or tape measure

Hole punch

## wrapping and packaging

✓ Use fabric in place of tissue paper to dress up a gift bag; clothe a wine bottle or quart jar; line a gift box (Chinese take-out containers being one of my favorites); or wrap a gift, using ribbon instead of adhesive tape to secure the package.

✓ Make cloth envelopes. I'm partial to presenting my aprons in pouches made from my old tablecloths, because I can customize the size of the pouch to the apron. Starting with, say, a 15-inch square, I'll either pink the edges or hem them (turn them in ¼-inch, iron, turn again, and topstitch). Then I draw three of the four corners to the center and secure them together by sewing on a button. The last corner becomes the flap.

## cards, envelopes, and albums

✓ Embellish card stock with a charming bit of recycled table linen or embroidered dish towel. Using pinking shears, cut a piece to fit the front of the card; I like to size the fabric so that ¼-inch of card frames it. Using the fabric as a template, cut a matching piece of iron-on vinyl and adhesive. Fuse the vinyl to the fabric; apply Wonder Under to the wrong side, peel off the protective film, and affix the fabric to the front of the card. Alternatively, machine-stitch the vinylized fabric to the card.

✓ Laminate a photo, or something cut out of a magazine, to the piece of fabric using the Therm O Web. Then mount on card stock or a photo album.

✓ Use this same technique to pretty-up a recipe file or index.

✓ Create gift tags. Use quilt templates, or make your own from cardboard, to cut the fabric into more interesting shapes. For instance, I use an octagon shape to create gift tags for, say, the neck of a bottle or a gift bag. (Once the layers are fused, I punch a hole at the top and run a ribbon through it.) This is a good way to recycle small scraps from your old linens.

## napkins, placemats, aprons, and bibs

✓ If you're able to salvage big enough squares—18 inches is a good size—simply hem the edges for dinner napkins.

✓ With smaller squares, and especially with a variety of patterns, create a set of dinner napkins by pinking the fabric edges and either stitching or fusing them onto purchased cloth napkins.

✓ Make place mats. If you can salvage large rectangles, waterproof them with the Therm O Web iron-on vinyl and hem the edges; I like to add rickrack before stitching all around (align the edge of the mat with the center of the rickrack). Otherwise, pink the edges of the salvaged fabric before vinylizing it, and then stitch or fuse it onto ready-made place mats. You can iron these mats after you wash them, provided you use a press cloth.

✓ Make bibs. Iron fabric remnants with the Therm O Web and cut out bibs. Hem the edges with binding, cutting the binding extra long to create the bib ties. I like to add rickrack to the edge, too.

✓ Napkins can double as flatware holders if you attach a 10-inch ribbon or length of twill to the right side, smack in the center of the napkin. With the wrong side up, roll up a knife/fork/spoon set as you would a burrito or blintz, and then tie the roll closed.

## sachets and storage bags

✓ Use overly stained napkins or tablecloth sections as protective layers for stacking good china.

✓ Make sachets. Sew two pieces of fabric, right sides together, around three sides; turn inside out, stuff with lavender or any other fragrant herb; turn in the fourth edge and slipstitch closed, or gather the open end and tie with a ribbon. Adorn with an old button.

✓ Make storage bags for comforters, quilts, and other bedding. Fold rectangular tablecloths in half, sew two sides; or sew two same-sized cloths together, right sides in, along three sides, and turn the bag right-side out.

## guest towels

✓ Using a purchased towel as a template, cut the fabric and hem the raw edges along the long sides. Finish the short sides with purchased trim, or sew an anchoring line of stitches ½-inch from the end and fray the fabric.

## coasters

✓ Therm-O-Web salvaged table linen and cut into coasters with pinking shears.

## electronic gadget covers

✓ Protect those precious electronics—MP3 players, wireless readers, mobile phones—with custom cloth covers from your old table linens!

1. Cut two pieces of fabric (one will become the lining) to the size of your gadget, adding ½- to ¾-inches all around for seam allowance and "give."
2. Sew the right sides together all around, ¼-inch from the outer edge, leaving an opening (at least 3 inches) on one long side for turning inside out.
3. Turn the bag inside out. Push out the corners and press the bag flat. Press down ¼-inch of the raw edges of the bag's opening (to make slipstitching them closed easier).
4. With the lining side facing down, bring the two short ends toward each other so they meet in the middle. Pin down.
5. Sew along the long sides, back and forth, ¼-inch from the edge. This creates two pockets. Turn the pockets inside out.
6. Slipstitch the bag opening closed.

# NOTES ON FABRIC CARE

**THE JOY** of having linens is in using them every day. Why not? Modern washing machines, with their many cycles and programs, have made it fairly easy to launder even delicate and hand-wash-only materials. Some of the stain pretreatments are terrific at lifting grease and wine, formerly the bane of household linens. I don't have a linen press, but my steam iron, provided I keep it clean of mineral deposits, does a great job.

In short, I don't see the point of getting nutty over the care and preservation of my cloths. I figure what kept these goods from being used in the first place was the stringency attached to their caretaking. Below, I've gathered some excellent advice, courtesy of the Good Housekeeping Research Institute, to help you restore, launder, dry, press, and store your cloths with ease. And should you experience a disaster—tearing a lace insert by getting too aggressive with the steam iron, as I did recently—bear in mind that there are literally tons of linens out there in the secondhand and antique stores, just waiting for someone to give them a good home.

*SAVE PAPER TOWEL inserts and roll your ironed-flat napkins onto them. Stored in this manner, they are ready for use without even a bit of touch-up. Tablecloths can be rolled onto empty wrapping paper cylinders.*

## LAUNDERING

Always wash whites and colors separately.

Soak vintage linens for 6 to 8 hours in a big tub (like your bathtub) in warm water and Restoration, the best product for removing overall yellowing and some stains (with the exception of blood).

Pretreat before soaking with some concentrated Restoration (follow manufacturer's instructions).

After soaking, pour off the water, rinse with warm water, and soak in distilled white vinegar for 2 hours. Rinse again with warm water.

Still have stains? Try this: Squeeze two lemons into a juicer. Double fold a towel under the stained linen. Spoon about 2 tablespoons of the juice onto the stain, and then rub in 1 teaspoon of salt. Let dry for a few hours and rinse with the vinegar. Do a final rinse with warm water.

If someone tells you that adding buttermilk to this process will help, don't believe her. According to Kathleen Huddy, director of textiles at *Good Housekeeping*, soaking linens in a buttermilk/vinegar/lemon juice solution "didn't work well at all and left the linens smelling awful!"

Old-timers are right about the stain-lifting powers of the sun, however. Sunlight is a natural fabric whitener. Sometimes a stain you've worked on unsuccessfully will magically disappear after 2 hours' sun therapy out on your lawn.

Make sure to rinse your linens thoroughly to remove all soap residue.

Hard water is an absolute no-no when washing linens. It contains minerals such as calcium and magnesium, which make the soap and/or detergent less effective. Hard water may explain why you find your linen to be stiff and dull with a line of soap scum on it after washing. Soft water is a much better option for washing linens. The soap or detergent will work more effectively and your linens will be soap-scum free! Use distilled water if you do not have soft water.

Vintage linens that do not carry a care instruction label can be laundered in your washing machine with a minimal amount of soap. Be sure to choose the delicate or hand-wash cycle. Cold temperatures are safest, although warm may give stain treatments a boost. Do not use hot. Hot water sets stains and shrinks fabric.

## DRYING

Linens washed by machine can be line- or machine-dried on a gentle cycle. Delicate, vintage linens should be rolled in terry towels and pressed upon to extract as much water as possible and then spread out on the lawn or draped over a line to dry. You'll have an easier time rolling them or folding them for storage if you bring them in ever-so-slightly damp. Make sure they're completely air-dried before tucking them away.

## STORING

Resist the urge to iron vintage linens that you're storing for any length of time. Ironing can create hard seams, which may cause cracks and creases that cannot be removed. Likewise, do not starch linens and then put them away. Starch can attract moths that will eat the starch along with the fibers that carry it.

Store linens dry, out of the light, and never in a damp place. Roll them loosely in acid-free tissue or clean cotton (old sheets and pillowcases are good). Loose rolling causes less stress on the fabric. Folding, like ironing, can create irremediable creases and lines. If the items are being stacked, place the heaviest at the bottom so creases don't form from the weight of the goods. If storing in wooden drawers, protect the linen from touching the wood, which can leach and stain the linen. Line drawers and shelves with acid-free paper or make sure the linen items are completely covered in cotton.

## linen care tips

- If a bit of linen is too fragile or delicate to use, frame it.

- Do not use bleach (including sun bleaching) on fragile, delicate linens.

- For white linens, you may use a nonchlorine bleaching agent, such as hydrogen peroxide or oxygen bleach.

- Do not wring wet or damp linens before drying, as this can break the fabric fibers.

## IRONING

You will want to iron cotton and linen napkins and tablecloths before use for extra crispness. Iron at a medium-to-hot setting with plenty of steam. Iron on the wrong side first, then on the right side, so as to bring out the utmost sheen. Do not apply the iron directly to areas that have delicate lace or cutwork. You could easily tear it.

To iron round tablecloths, start at the center and work outward, turning the cloth as you go.

To iron rectangular tablecloths, fold in half lengthwise and iron first on the wrong side, until half dry, and then refold and iron until nearly dry on the right side.

Iron napkins flat; do not iron in the creases, which may result in creases that cannot be removed.

Iron damask fabric on both sides, wrong side first.

Iron pure linen when it's damp.

*IRONING IS THE opportunity to daydream, talk out loud, sing along to a CD, listen to a book on tape, and experience the joy of the mundane.*

VEGETABLE POLK

# RESOURCES AND
# RECOMMENDED READING

Barineau, Yvonne, and Erin Henderson. *Colorful Tablecloths 1930s–1960s: Threads of the Past.* Atglen, Pennsylvania: Schiffer Publishing Ltd., 2004.

Brobeck, Florence. *How to Give Luncheons, Teas, and Showers.* Garden City, New York: Nelson Doubleday, Inc., 1964.

Caplin, Jessie F. *The Lace Book.* New York: The Macmillan Company, 1932.

Davidson, Alan. *The Oxford Companion to Food.* New York: Oxford University Press, 1999.

de Bonneville, Françoise. *The Book of Fine Linen.* Paris: Flammarion, 1994.

Fehling, Loretta Smith. *More Terrific Tablecloths.* Atglen, Pennsylvania: Schiffer Publishing Ltd., 1999.

_____. *Terrific Tablecloths from the '40s & '50s.* Atglen, Pennsylvania: Schiffer Publishing Ltd., 1998.

Foley, Tricia. *Linens and Lace.* New York: Clarkson Potter, 1990.

Glasell, Pamela. *Collectors' Guide to Vintage Tablecloths.* Atglen, Pennsylvania: Schiffer Publishing Ltd., 2002.

Hayes, Michelle. *Fun and Collectible Kitchen Towels*. Atglen, Pennsylvania: Schiffer Publishing Ltd., 2005.

Henderson, Erin, and Yvonne Barineau. *Colorful Vintage Kitchen Towels*. Atglen, Pennsylvania: Schiffer Publishing Ltd., 2006.

Manchester, Marsha L. *Antique Linens from the Kitchen to the Boudoir*. Atglen, Pennsylvania: Schiffer Publishing Ltd., 2003.

Mendelson, Cheryl. *Home Comforts: The Art & Science of Keeping House*. New York: Scribner, 1999.

Miller, Susan. *Vintage Feed Sacks: Fabric from the Farm*. Atglen, Pennsylvania: Schiffer Publishing Ltd., 2007.

Roberts, Patricia Easterbrook. *Table Settings, Entertaining, and Etiquette: A History and Guide*. New York: Viking Press, 1967.

Rosen, Lynn. *Elements of the Table: A Simple Guide for Hosts and Guests*. New York: Clarkson Potter, 2007.

# ACKNOWLEDGMENTS

IN 1999, curious about the women who had once tied on an apron as daily domestic armor, I set out to learn their stories and collect their wisdom. What began as a solitary journey turned into a grassroots movement, led by the readers of *The Apron Book*. It is to y'all that I dedicate this book. Thank you for supporting my writing and embracing the notion that *aprons don't hold us back, they take us back.*

With *The Kitchen Linens Book*, I've delved even deeper into our collective domestic past, spotlighting the women whose handiwork turned the utilitarian cloths of daily life into canvases of personal expression. How lucky I am to have my creative team, Lisa DiMona and Melinda Marshall of Lark Productions, and Patty Rice, my editor at Andrews McMeel, enable my infatuation with initialed napkins, embroidered dish towels, colorful table coverings, and vintage hot pads! From aprons to linens—who knew? Thank you for once again turning my vision into published reality.

My sincerest thanks as well to Andrews McMeel's senior art director Julie Barnes, designer Diane Marsh, and production editor Caty Neis for designing yet another beautiful book for me; Tammie Barker, my publicist at Andrews McMeel, for being one-in-a-million; Kathleen Huddy, director of textiles at *Good Housekeeping*, for sharing her vintage-care research; and Ellen Levine, editorial director of Hearst Publications, for continuing to embrace my passions.

I am grateful to the McCall Pattern Company for allowing me to share their adorable vintage transfer, and to Winkie Rhea of Consumer Services for her help in this endeavor.

I am not alone in my love of vintage linens. I am so very grateful to the following for sharing with me their knowledge of thread and fabric, their collections of cloth goods, and their stories within the weave: Karen Smith, Mariella Warner, Mary Tonne, Katherine Frame, Marsha See, Grace Brown, Cynthia Daddona, Molly Dunham, Karin Kimball

Smith, Dora Beeman, Priscilla Esser, Carol Nash, Kay Christensen, Michelle Tomky, Laura Kelley, Lynda Lorenz, Suzanne Straha, Sheryl-lyn Walz, Patty Bedard, Kim Tapsfield, Betty Faye Ortiz, and Carolyn Gilbert.

My appreciation further extends to Steve Bigley of APS Photography in Pueblo, Colorado, and David and Paula Morris, David Morris Photography in Kansas City, Missouri, for their attention to detail when photographing my collections; my friend Mary Bonogofsky for accepting my invitation to steam, starch, and iron all the linens photographed; Catherine Hopkinson-Higley of Savannah Photography, Pueblo, for my pretty author photo; Earl Downs for letting me use the cherished snapshot of his mother, Virginia, as the portal to this book; and the Carolina Sauce Company in Durham, North Carolina, for providing substitutions to my beloved Boar and Castle.

And a special acknowledgment to Else Frank Geisel, who embroidered the dish towel featured on *The Kitchen Linens Book* cover. Were she still with us, she would express her delight with a sweet smile. In her absence, Hank—her son and my prince charming—will do so.

# index

## PROJECTS AND RECIPES

# CREDITS

**STEVE BIGLEY, APS PHOTOGRAPHY:** title page, vi, 2, 5, 7, 8, 9, 10, 12, 13, 18, 19, 23, 24, 25, 26, 28, 31, 35, 36, 39, 40, 41, 44, 46, 47, 50, 51, 52, 53, 54, 55, 56, 57, 59, 61, 62, 63, 64, 65, 68, 70, 71, 73, 74, 75, 76, 80, 81, 82, 83, 84, 85, 86, 87, 88, 91, 92, 93, 100, 105, 106, 107, 108, 109, 112, 113, 114, 115, 119, 124, 136

**ELLYNANNE GEISEL:** 130

**CATHERINE HOPKINSON-HIGLEY, SAVANNAH PHOTOGRAPHY:** 38, author photo

**DAVID MORRIS, DAVID MORRIS PHOTOGRAPHY:** 11, 15, 16, 20, 27, 29, 30, 32, 33, 34, 43, 45, 48, 49, 66, 95, 96, 103, 104, 110, 116, 120, 127, 134, 137, 138

**P. 5:** photo courtesy of Earl Downs

**P. 30, 36, 68, 70, 75, 96, 97, 98, 118, 124, 125:** from the author's collection

**P. 44:** exquisite handwork courtesy of Warner's Antiques by Mariella, www.warnersantiques.com